A Brief Guide to
Brief Therapy

A Brief Guide to
Brief Therapy

Brian Cade
William Hudson O'Hanlon

W. W. NORTON & COMPANY · *NEW YORK* · LONDON

Printed in the United States of America.

The text of this book was composed in Century Textbook. Composition
by Bytheway Typesetting Services, Inc. Manufacturing by Haddon
Craftsmen, Inc.

Library of Congress Cataloging-in-Publication Data

Cade, Brian.
  A brief guide to brief therapy / Brian Cade, William Hudson
O'Hanlon.
    p. cm.
  "A Norton professional book" – P. facing t.p.
  Includes bibliographical references and index.
  ISBN 0-393-70143-3
  1. Brief psychotherapy – Handbooks, manuals, etc.   I. O'Hanlon,
William Hudson.   II. Title.
  [DNLM: 1. Psychotherapy, Brief – methods.   WM 420 C122b]
RC480.55.C33   1993
616.89′14 – dc20
DNLM/DLC   92-48864 CIP
for Library of Congress

W.W. Norton & Company, Inc., 500 Fifth Avenue, New York, N.Y. 10110
W.W. Norton & Company, Ltd., 10 Coptic Street, London WC1A 1PU

      6 7 8 9 0

We would both like to dedicate this book to

our respective families. Neither of us understands

why the hell they put up with us.

CONTENTS

vii

ACKNOWLEDGMENTS

We would like to acknowledge the help of our friend and colleague, Michael Durrant, for his valuable advice, his support, his regular admonishment to "get on with it," his frequent and welcome offers of a glass of wine (offered to Brian, not to Bill, who lived far too far away), and, finally, for his expertise with computers.

We would also like to express our thanks to the editors of the respective journals who gave their permission for us to reproduce or to adapt the whole or parts of the following papers:

Cade, B. (1982). Some uses of metaphor. *The Australian Journal of Family Therapy, 3*: 135–140.
Cade, B. (1984). Paradoxical techniques in therapy. *Journal of Child Psychology and Psychiatry, 25*: 509–516.
Cade, B. (1986). The reality of "reality" (or the "reality" of reality). *The American Journal of Family Therapy, 14*: 49–56.
Cade, B. (1987). Brief/strategic approaches to therapy: A commentary. *The Australian and New Zealand Journal of Family Therapy, 8*: 37–44.
Cade, B. (1988). The art of neglecting children: Passing the responsibility back. *Family Therapy Case Studies, 3*: 27–34.
Cade, B. (1989). Over-responsibility and under-responsibility: Opposite sides of the coin. *A celebration of family ther-*

apy—10th anniversary issue of The Journal of Family Therapy, Spring: 103–121.

Cade, B. (1992). A response by any other. . . . *Journal of Family Therapy, 14*: 163–169.

Cade, B. (1992). I am an unashamed expert. *Context: A News Magazine of Family Therapy*, Summer, 30–31.

Cade, B., & Seligman, P. (1981). Nothing is good or bad but thinking makes it so. *The Association for Child Psychology and Psychiatry: Newsletter*, No. 6, Spring: 4–7.

Finally, we would like to thank Susan Barrows Munro of Norton for her infinite patience and understanding and for her good humor, the quality of which must, at times, have been strained. And to her new assistant, Margaret Farley, we would like to express our admiration for the rapid development of her skills in "brief editing."

PREFACE

The authors first met in Cardiff, Wales, in the early 1980s. Bill was presenting a workshop that had been sponsored by The Family Institute where Brian was then employed. We found that we had much in common. We both played the guitar and had written songs. We had once grown long hair (a commodity Brian has now become somewhat short of) and had worn floral shirts and beads. We discovered that we thought about and practiced brief therapy in ways that had much in common, though also with some differences in emphasis. We both saw Milton Erickson as having had a most important influence on the development of our ways of practicing and thinking about therapy, although only Bill had actually met him.

Fairly early in our relationship, we decided to collaborate on a book that would summarize the main elements, the ideas, principles, attitudes, and techniques associated with brief therapy. We had each been practicing and teaching the approach since the mid 1970s and felt we had something significant to say. The book would reflect both the similarities and the differences in our work.

Somehow the book took longer to write than we had thought it would. This was partly because the field (and we) kept on developing faster than we could keep up with; partly because we are both busy people; partly because we were both writing too many other things; partly because Brian suddenly emigrated to Australia; partly because . . . and so on. The project finally took off when, by accident, we discovered that we had both purchased compatible computers and compatible word-processor programs, and that we now both had fax machines.

A problem then emerged that we had not earlier anticipated. What was it that we now did in therapy, and how did we now think about it? In the heady days of the late seventies and the early eighties, we, along with most of our brief/strategic colleagues, dealt in relative certainties. We were good tacticians, working from clear process-focused ideas about how problems evolved and were maintained, had boundless energy and enthusiasm and a veritable cornucopia of clever ideas for interventions.

We are now less certain, less audaciously tactical, less wedded to over-simplistic models, and far less impressed with our own cleverness. We have become more concerned with the resourcefulness of our clients and with avoiding approaches that disempower, either overtly or covertly. We have become more concerned with the development of a cooperative approach. However, we remain somewhat skeptical about the sanctimonious way that some of our colleagues are denying the validity of professional expertise and asserting that it is both possible and desirable to avoid exercising any form of influence. While we believe it is impossible not to influence, " . . . there is a way to be open to clients influencing you as a therapist. You can listen to them instead of your theories. You can validate their experience and let them teach you what works and doesn't work for them" (O'Hanlon, 1991, p. 109).

Clearly, it would have been much easier for us if we had written this book when the idea first occurred to us and while we were still enjoying a considerable degree of certainty about what we were thinking and about what we were doing. Hopefully this might turn out, however, to be a more useful book.

INTRODUCTION

Over the past three decades, considerably influenced by the publication in 1963 of Jay Haley's *Strategies of Psychotherapy* and by the subsequent work of the Brief Therapy Center, Palo Alto (Watzlawick et al., 1974; Weakland et al., 1974), there has been a rapid growth in interest in the development of brief/ strategic approaches to therapy. In contrast to most of the models that then prevailed, a more active, directive approach evolved that viewed therapy primarily as about promoting change rather than promoting growth, understanding or insight, the therapist becoming much more instrumental as an agent in the process of bringing about change.

Much of the early impetus behind the development of this approach was an interest in innovation and in the discovery of better techniques for bringing about change. Over the ensuing years, it became increasingly clear that the duration of successful therapy could be much shorter than was expected by practitioners operating within the tenets of the more traditional approaches. Increasing numbers of practitioners and teams throughout the world became fascinated by, and started experimenting with, the approach. They were attracted by the optimism and the pragmatic focus, the creativity as well as the contribution to effective therapy. There followed an exponential swell of professional papers, chapters, and books elaborating an increasing wealth of ideas and techniques. More recently, the possibility of brief but effective forms of intervention has become popular with various funding sources, insurance companies, and the many beleaguered helping agencies struggling to provide services to increasing numbers of clients in a climate of rapidly diminishing financial resources.

Over recent years, however, a more sober and critical look is beginning to be taken at the approach, at the implications of many of the techniques that have been developed, and at some of the underlying assumptions that have been guiding the practice of brief therapy or, alternatively, that it has been accused of having ignored or neglected. The approach has always had its outside critics, but now the field is itself taking a more careful look at the direction in which it had been traveling and at where it is now headed.

Among the main areas of concern appear to be:

- the use of covert and manipulative techniques (for example, paradoxical interventions), particularly where these involve covert agendas on the part of the therapist or team and, at times, varying degrees of deliberate deception;
- the implicit or explicit abuse of the therapist's position of power and control in defining direction and outcome, particularly where this remains outside of the awareness of the client;
- the narrow, largely pragmatic, and behavioral focus taken by the approach and its apparent lack of concern with the intrapsychic or emotional variables in a client's life;
- the somewhat cavalier approach that appears to be taken to the importance or existence of an identifiable reality or truth in human affairs;
- the failure to address seriously the sociopolitical variables affecting a client's life, particularly those relating to gender.

Throughout the course of this book, we will touch upon many of these themes, though we do not necessarily promise to resolve all of the dilemmas raised. We do not wish to deny that brief therapists have, at times, presented themselves as somewhat narrowly focused and adversarial and tricky in their work, sometimes unashamedly so. However, we believe that good brief therapists have always listened carefully to their clients' concerns (including respecting their feelings), have considered their wider contextual constraints, and have operated from a position of respect for a client's own resources. We also believe that the field has evolved significantly since those heady, reckless days in the early 1970s when writings neglected to mention these factors.

We agree with Steve de Shazer, who, when asked about the manipulative/unethical reputation that brief therapists had gained for themselves, responded:

> We have found that there is no need to invent some of those tricky things, the deceptive things that some of us used to do in the past. Our fancy techniques are now all above board and we are using material given to us by the family. In fact, looking back, I guess that all those techniques came from the families we worked with. I think the concerns that some people have arise out of the way we authors wrote about what we were doing, and we wrote about it in such a way that it might not / recover. If we had written it differently we could have said, "Look, my, ain't those clients clever!!" (Cade, 1985b, p. 97)

We no longer use the systemic paradigm as our main model. It is the individual *only* who can act and react to circumstances. We prefer the term *interactional* to the term *systemic*, in that the former leads one to consider repetitive and potentially observable processes in which people are reacting sequentially to each other. The latter can be too static and also lacking in specificity, as well as lending itself to reification.

We are also guided, both for pragmatic as well as aesthetic reasons, by Occam's principle of parsimony. Brother William of Occam, an English philosopher of the fourteenth century, held that the fewest assumptions should be made when explaining any phenomenon. Working from the principle that "It is vain to do with more what can be achieved with fewer," he dissected every framework as though with a razor. As further explained by Bertrand Russell, " . . . if everything in some science can be interpreted without assuming this or that hypothetical entity there is no ground for assuming it" (Russell, 1979, p. 462).

Following an historical overview, we plan to give the reader a reasonably comprehensive tour around various aspects of the field, as we currently see it. (Bill originally wanted to call the book, *A Hitchhiker's Guide to Brief Therapy*, but Brian's British reserve finally prevailed.) It will certainly not be a totally exhaustive tour nor, hopefully, an exhausting one. We have avoided a cookbook approach, though there will be some cookbook-like sections. We have avoided writing a totally theoretical textbook, though we certainly do intersperse some theory.

We hope this book will reflect the current trend toward a markedly and transparently more cooperative and respectful approach. We also hope we are successful in communicating our continued excitement about and commitment to the potentials of the brief approaches while, at the same time, minimizing or avoiding the crusader's fundamentalist zeal that might have crept in had we written the book when we initially planned to.

We would like to make clear at the outset that the "brief therapy" we are talking about derives from the tradition of family therapy and the work of Milton Erickson. There is another branch of "brief therapy" that derives from Freud and the psychodynamic tradition, which is usually considerably more lengthy than the therapy we describe here. We write this to ensure that you have wandered into the right book, rather like the flight attendants announcing the destination of the airplane before the doors close. If this kind of brief therapy is not your desired destination, this a good time to deplane.

A Brief Guide to
Brief Therapy

1

BRIEF/STRATEGIC APPROACHES TO THERAPY: AN OVERVIEW

Were I asked to explain strategic psychotherapy standing on one leg . . . I would answer, "Patients attempt to master their problems with a strategy which, because it is unsuccessful, the therapist changes. All the rest is commentary."

—Rabkin (1977, p. 5)

Milton H. Erickson, M.D., was the first strategic therapist. He might even be called the first therapist, since he was the first major clinician to concentrate on how to change people.

—Haley (1985, p. vii)

EARLY HISTORY:
SOME IMPORTANT MILESTONES

It is not possible to underestimate the influence of Milton Erickson on the development of the brief/strategic approaches. His attitudes and his inventive genius were of considerable influence during the early development of the communications approaches centered initially on the work of the Gregory Bateson research project. This was set up in 1952 to look at the paradoxes of abstraction in communication utilizing the theory of logical types (Whitehead & Russell, 1910–13). Bateson was joined on this project by John Weakland, Jay Haley, and William Fry, Jr. Other important early influences were the work of Norbert Weiner on cybernetics, the developing science of communication and control in systems (Weiner, 1948), and the work of Shannon and Weaver developing a mathematics of information exchange and information flow (1949).

At the same time, Don Jackson, a psychiatrist, was developing his ideas on family homeostasis (1975). He began working closely with the Bateson research group and was subsequently to become a member. "Data of various types were used in the research: Hypnosis, ventriloquism, animal training, popular moving pictures, the nature of play, humor, schizophrenia, neurotic communication, psychotherapy, family systems and family therapy" (Haley, 1963, p. ix).

Over the ten years' duration of this project its members made many visits to consult with Milton Erickson to discuss aspects of hypnosis and therapy and also to receive supervision on their own cases. Transcripts of many of these consultations have recently been published in three volumes edited by Jay Haley (1985).

In 1956, the classic and seminal paper *Toward a Theory of Schizophrenia* was published, elaborating the double-bind theory of the etiology of schizophrenia (Bateson et al., 1956).

In 1958, Don Jackson founded the Mental Research Institute (MRI) in Palo Alto, California, and was joined by John Weakland, Jay Haley, Jules Riskin, Virginia Satir, and Paul Watzlawick. George Greenberg has written an excellent tribute to the influence and ideas of Don Jackson (Greenberg, 1977).

In 1963, Haley published his brilliant book, *Strategies of Psychotherapy*, which highlighted the paradoxical nature of all therapy and which also demonstrated the influence of Milton Erickson on his thinking.

In 1966, Richard Fisch started the brief therapy project within the MRI, which was to have a profound effect on the development of brief/strategic approaches.

Two important works appeared in 1967: Haley's paper, *Toward a Theory of Pathological Systems*, which was concerned with the influence of crossgenerational coalitions (the perverse triangle) in the development of pathology (Haley, 1967a), and the book *Pragmatics of Human Communication: A Study of Interactional Patterns, Pathologies, and Paradoxes* (Watzlawick, Beavin, & Jackson, 1967).

In 1967, Haley moved to the Philadelphia Child Guidance Clinic, where he joined Salvador Minuchin and Braulio Montalvo and became increasingly concerned with structure and hierarchy. In 1973 *Uncommon Therapy: The Psychiatric Techniques of Milton H. Erickson* was published, in which Haley introduced the term "strategic therapy" and elaborated his ideas on Erickson's approach to problems as occurring throughout the various stages of the family life cycle. As Lynn Hoffman observes, this book represents the culmination of Haley's earlier concern with process. She points out, "In writing about strategic therapy, Haley stays mainly with process language. After he decided to join Minuchin in Philadelphia . . . he began to downplay the use of hypnotic techniques and paradoxical directives (although by no means abandoning his sense of their importance), and concentrated on a more organizational model for therapy" (Hoffman, 1981, p. 280). Haley's shift from a concern with process to a concern with form is clearly demonstrated in his later works, *Problem Solving Therapy* (1976) and *Leaving Home: The Therapy of Disturbed Young People* (1980b).

In 1971, Mara Selvini Palazzoli, Luigi Boscolo, Gianfranco Cecchin, and Guiliana Prata began working together in Milan and in 1974 published a paper, *The Treatment of Children Through the Brief Therapy of Their Parents*. Though some authors include their approach as one of the brief/strategic approaches (Stanton, 1981), Hoffman has observed that "The Milan Associates, although influenced by the Palo Alto group, evolved in a quite different direction, creating a form unique and distinct enough to be considered a school of its own" (Hoffman, 1981, p. 285). We agree with Hoffman's observation and do not include the Milan Associates as being within the "brief/strategic" approaches, while acknowledging the tactical brilliance of their work and the influence that their way of thinking, their concern with context, their style of interviewing, and their use of systemic "paradoxical" interventions has had on many brief/strategic therapists.

In 1974, two important works were published by members of the MRI brief therapy project, the book *Change: Principles of Problem Formation and Problem Resolution* (Watzlawick et al., 1974) and the paper *Brief Therapy: Focused Problem Resolution* (Weakland et al., 1974). These works had an immediate and dramatic impact on the field of family therapy and contributed profoundly to the subsequent rapid spread of interest in brief/strategic approaches. This group has continued to refine its ideas about therapy, its subsequent work concentrating far less on elaborating theory and more on the pragmatics of brief, problem-focused therapy (Fisch et al., 1982).

One other early figure of importance is Richard Rabkin, whose unique style is demonstrated in *Strategic Psychotherapy: Brief and Symptomatic Treatment* (1977), in which he uses a chess analogy, dividing the stages of therapy into the opening, the midgame, and the endgame.

DEFINITIONS

Haley defined strategic therapy as follows:

> Therapy can be called strategic if the clinician initiates what happens during the therapy and designs a particular approach for each problem. . . . [The therapist] must identify solvable problems, set goals, design interventions to achieve those goals, examine the responses he receives to correct his approach, and ultimately examine the outcome of his therapy to see if it has been effective. The therapist must be acutely sensitive and responsive to the patient and his social field, but how he proceeds must be determined by himself. (Haley, 1973, p. 17)

Richard Rabkin differentiated the strategic approaches from those therapies that "seek wisdom and enlightenment," defining them as "usually brief" and concerned with "changing the approach that patients have toward their problems and symptoms" (1977, pp. 6–7).

Weakland et al. use the term "brief therapy" rather than strategic to describe their approach (Weakland et al., 1974), as did Peggy Papp (1983), a term that is considered by Rabkin as "not specific enough" (1977, p. 7).

Typical of the brief/strategic therapist is the avoidance of an elaborate theory of personality or of dysfunction, whether it be at the individual, family, or wider system level. Diagnostic formulations tend to represent the most simplified way, in each case, of thinking about the evolution and maintenance of problems that will allow an effective way of intervening to be developed. Brief/strategic therapists are concerned with how to intervene as briefly and as economically as possible, and with a continuing exploration of and elaboration of those therapist behaviors and attitudes that tend to maximize the facilitation of rapid problem resolution.

Through the more recent writings of Jay Haley and of Cloé Madanes the term "strategic therapy" has become much more associated with their structural/hierarchical/power-focused concerns in therapy. Thus, in subsequent chapters, we will be using the term "brief" rather than "strategic" to refer to the primarily process-focused approaches that will be the concern of the bulk of this book.

Brief therapy is essentially concerned with observable phenomena, is pragmatic and related to the belief that problems are produced and maintained

1. by the constructs through which difficulties are viewed (Kelly, 1955), and
2. by repetitive behavioral sequences (both personal and interpersonal) surrounding them. These can, of course, include the constructs and inputs of therapists.

THE TWO MAIN APPROACHES

Though all brief/strategic therapists would agree on the importance of identifying repetitive behavioral sequences, the brief/strategic approaches can be divided into two main groupings in terms of how the information tends to be used:

a. Those (which we will define as strategic therapies) that are concerned with how repetitive sequences reveal and reflect form. Symptoms are usually seen as serving a function in the family and as carrying metaphorical information about hierarchical dysfunction (Haley, 1976; Madanes, 1981a, 1984; Papp, 1983). Sequences are observed in order to map out a family's organization.

b. Those (which we will define as brief therapies) for whom an analysis of the ideas and the repetitive sequences surrounding symptoms is a sufficient level of explanation, and inferences about purpose, function, or family structure are seen as unnecessary (Cade, 1985; de Shazer, 1982, 1985, 1988; Fisch et al., 1982; O'Hanlon, 1982; O'Hanlon & Weiner-Davis, 1989; Weakland et al., 1974). Sequences are observed in order to identify self-reinforcing patterns of thought and behavior.

Approaches Concerned with Form and Function

Haley's approach, as outlined in *Problem Solving Therapy* (1976), is based on the belief that symptoms are the sign of a system in which the hierarchical arrangement is either constantly ambiguous or involves repeated coalitions across generational or organizational boundaries. Such ambiguity or confusion is mapped by observing the repetitive ways that the members of the system deal with one another, particularly in respect to the problem behavior. For example, a parent may be exasperated by a child, yet continually protect the child from the spouse's attempts to help discipline, while at the same time he or she may express anger or desperation and demand such help. Alternatively, a grandparent can constantly collude with a child against, or protect it from, its parents, and thus undermine their attempts to encourage or enforce what they consider to be appropriate behaviors. At the same time, he or she can blame the child's disturbed behaviors on the parents' incompetence or indifference. Problems tend to be more severe where the hierarchical confusion is covert and/or denied. Therapy, from this perspective, involves changing these sequences such that the hierarchy is corrected and the ambiguity or confusion is diminished. Madanes comments:

> Parents are expected to be in charge of their children, and cross generational coalitions, such as one parent siding with a child against another parent, are blocked. There is also a cautious concern about where the therapist is in the hierarchy, so that he or she does not inadvertently form coalitions with members low in the hierarchy against those who are higher. (Madanes, 1981b, p. 22)

Symptoms are seen as a metaphorical communication about a more fundamental problem as well as a dysfunctional solution to that problem. They are seen as contracts between people or tactics in power struggles. As Madanes comments:

> In the case of a depressed man who does not do his work, it would be assumed that this is the way that the man and his wife (and/or his mother, father, children, and others) communicate about some specific issues, such as whether the wife appreciates her husband and his work, or whether the husband should do what his wife or his mother wishes, or so on. It is possible that the couple could become unstable over the presenting problem and that then a child might develop a symptom which will keep the father actively involved taking care of the child rather than depressed and incompetent. (Madanes, 1981b, p. 21)

Thus, in this approach, symptoms are seen as having protective or stabilizing functions. Papp talks of keeping questions in mind such as, "What function does the symptom serve in stabilizing the family?" and "What is the central theme around which the problem is organized?" She talks of changes in the life cycle of a family activating "conflicts that have been lying dormant, and these conflicts, rather than being resolved, are expressed through a symptom" (Papp, 1983, pp. 18–19). The purpose of the symptom is seen as either defending the family against changes or, alternatively, helping such changes be negotiated by forcing the family to reorganize.

Approaches That Focus on Process and Feedback Loops

The MRI brief therapy model is based on the belief that problems develop from, and are maintained by, the way that normal life difficulties are perceived and tackled either by the individual or by other involved people. Attempted solutions that derive from a particular belief framework applied to a difficulty can result in no change or in an exacerbation of the difficulty. A problem evolves as "more of the same" solutions, or classes of solutions, are repeatedly or increasingly applied or intensified leading to "more of the same" problem, in turn, leading to "more of the same" attempted solutions, and so on . . . (Watzlawick et al., 1974). Thus, problems are seen as being maintained by the continued application of these "wrong" or unsuccessful attempted solutions, which then become the problem. Of course, the same phenomenon can occur in therapy as "more of the same" therapeutic approach or class of techniques deriving from a particular framework or model can lead to "more of the same" problem, and so on. . . . An underreaction to or denial of a difficulty can also be an "attempted solution" that can perpetuate that difficulty and turn it into a problem.

The repeated application of "wrong" or unsuccessful solutions, then, locks the difficulty into a self-reinforcing pattern, which maintains the status quo. For example, the members of The Brief Therapy Center refer to the common pattern that develops between a depressed person and his intimates:

> The more they try to cheer him up and make him see the positive sides of life, the more depressed the patient is likely to get: "They don't even understand me." The action meant to *alleviate* the behavior of the other party *aggravates* it; the "cure" becomes worse than the original "disease." Unfortunately, this usually remains unnoted by those involved and even is disbelieved if anyone else tries to point it out. (Weakland et al., 1974, p. 149)

A parent's attempts to control a teenager drive him or her to further acts of rebellion, which elicit further attempts to control, and so on. An insomniac tries harder and harder to sleep, a phenomenon that can only occur spontaneously, and thus the frantic effort to sleep becomes the very reason why sleep is so elusive. In this approach, chronicity is seen as the persistence of a repeatedly mishandled difficulty. No inferences are made about underlying individual or family dysfunction. No purpose or function is attributed to symptoms. Concepts such as homeostasis, mental illness, or the interpersonal advantages of symptoms are not considered necessary or useful.

Fisch et al. comment that:

> people often persist in actions that maintain problems inadvertently, and often with the best of intentions. . . . They follow poor maps very carefully, and this is quite expectable for people who are understandably anxious in the midst of difficulties. Belief in such maps also make it hard to see that they are not serving as effective guides. . . . (1982, pp. 16–18)

Therapy with this approach is focused on the "attempted solutions," on stopping or even reversing the usual treatment that has served to exacerbate the situation, however logical that treatment appears to be. The assumption is that, once the feedback loops maintaining the problem are blocked, a greater range of behavior becomes available.

In contrast with the conventional wisdom, "If at first you don't succeed, try, try, again," Fisch et al. offer their view that "if at first you don't succeed, you might perhaps try a second time – but if you don't succeed then, try something different" (p. 18). They sum up their approach as follows:

> If problem formation and maintenance are seen as parts of a vicious-cycle process, in which well-intentioned solution behaviors maintain the problem, then alteration of these behaviors should interrupt the cycle and initiate resolution of the problem – that is, the cessation of the problem behavior, since it is no longer being provoked by other behaviors in the system of interaction. (1982, p. 18)

Thus "less of the same" can lead to "less of the same," and so on.

THERAPEUTIC INTERVENTION

Though the different brief/strategic approaches work from some different basic assumptions, there are many ways of intervening that are common to all brief therapists. As implied earlier, brief therapists are identified more by how they act than by their theoretical formulations. Milton Erickson seemed more to work from an implicit theory of intervention than from a clearly articulated theory of personality or of dysfunction. Lankton and Lankton have drawn up a list of principles underpinning Erickson's idiosyncratic approach. These can be seen as implicit in the work of most brief therapists.

1. People operate out of their internal maps and not out of sensory experience.
2. People make the best choice for themselves at any given moment.
3. The explanation, theory, or metaphor used to relate facts about a person is not the person.
4. Respect all messages from the client.
5. Teach choice; never attempt to take choice away.
6. The resources the client needs lie within his or her own personal history.
7. Meet the client at his or her model of the world.
8. The person with the most flexibility or choice will be the controlling element in the system.
9. A person can't not communicate.
10. If it's hard work, reduce it down.
11. Outcomes are determined at the psychological level. (Lankton & Lankton, 1983, p. 12)

Erickson's genius at constructing unique, often brilliant, interventions has become legendary. As important, in our opinion, was the profound respect he shared for his patients, his respect for their beliefs, for their capacity to change however chronic or acute their problems, and his concern with protecting their integrity.

Therapy is addressed to any or all of the following:

a. Modifying the client/family belief frameworks or constructs that can be seen as relating to the way difficulties are being perceived, approached, and maintained.
b. Modifying the repetitive sequences surrounding the problem, which derive from those frameworks.
c. Modifying therapist positions and approaches, which become part of a self-reinforcing pattern between therapist and client/family.
d. Modifying the relationship between client/family (and maybe the therapist) and wider family/neighborhood or professional systems.

Patterns as Habits

The brief approach assumes that people do the best they can given their situations and the constraints of the constructs (Kelly, 1955) through which they have come to view their difficulties (see Chapter 2). It is not assumed that symptoms reflect hypothetical underlying unresolved issues. The approach is not based on a deficit model. It is the authors' opinion that the majority of problems are embedded in habits of reaction and response, which are not necessarily more complex than, for example, a smoking or nail-biting habit, even though the ramifications of the habits may be much more far-reaching in their consequences. Also, just as a person might begin smoking heavily as a response to a particularly stressful period in their life and then find the habit hard to break, even though the stressful period is long past, so habitual emotional and behavioral reactions and responses that become part of problem contexts may similarly be seen as habits that may have long outlived the original stimuli that may have triggered them. Like many habits these are often hard to break, because of the self-reinforcing cycles in which they become caught up. It is, in our view, not necessary to infer a more fundamental, deeper substratum of unresolved issues, unconscious motivations, resistances, etc.

Life Stages

Therapists concerned with form see symptoms as an indication that a family is failing to move successfully from one stage to the next in the family life cycle. Therapy is supposed to help families to negotiate such a transition and to reorganize appropriately for the next stage. Particularly difficult can be those stages where someone is either added to or subtracted from the system – for example, birth, divorce, death, and when children grow up and begin to leave home (Haley, 1973, 1980b).

Therapists concerned with process also see such transition points as important. Fisch et al. comment:

> Problems begin from some ordinary life difficulty, of which there is never any shortage. The difficulty may stem from an unusual or fortuitous event. More often, though, the beginning is likely to be a common difficulty associated with one of the transitions regularly experienced in the course of life. (1982, p. 13)

The process of how the situation comes to be viewed and becomes inadvertently mishandled through the repeated application of unsuccessful solutions can escalate such a difficulty rapidly into a problem "whose eventual size and nature may have little apparent similarity to the original difficulty" (p. 14).

Change in What?

As suggested earlier, all brief/strategic approaches, whether their concern is with process or form, see change as arising out of the breaking of patterns, both of thought and action, the interruption of repeating sequences.

They also interest themselves directly with the presenting problem, even though their opinions on what it reflects or represents might differ significantly. As Haley observes:

> by focusing on the symptoms the therapist gains the most leverage and has the most opportunity for bringing about change. It is the presenting problem that most interests the

client: when the therapist works with that he can gain great cooperation. . . . The goal is not to teach the family about their malfunctioning system, but to change the family sequences so that the presenting problems are resolved. (1976, p. 129)

Therapists concerned with process focus their attention on attempted solutions, intending to block or reverse them. For example:

A man sought help, having found himself increasingly unable to maintain an erection. This was causing him considerable distress and creating some tension in his relationship with his girlfriend. They were seen conjointly and the man told he needed to learn how to control the behavior of his penis more effectively. As the first step toward his learning this control, the girl was asked, that night, to try all she could to make him excited. He was instructed to try to prevent his penis becoming or staying erect. He failed. (Cade, 1979, p. 92)

Weakland et al. also remark:

We contend generally that change can be effected most easily if the goal of change is reasonably small and clearly stated. Once the patient has experienced a small but definite change in the seemingly monolithic nature of the problem most real to him, the experience leads to further, self-induced changes in this, and often also, in other areas of his life. That is, beneficient circles are initiated. (1974, p. 150)

Therapists concerned with form tend to plan their therapy in stages and focus directly on the family's dysfunctional organization. Often, the family is shifted to a different dysfunctional organization as a first step on the way to a more functional one. For example, a pattern including an over-involved parent might be moved to one in which the other, more peripheral parent must make all of the important decisions about the children as an initial step, before moving both parents to act together more effectively. Assignments given to families in respect of such goals tend to be followed up in subsequent sessions with some vigor.

Therapists concerned with process, though they put considerable thought into the planning of interventions, do not operate from a normative position on how families ought to be organized and, thus, tend to take each new session as it comes. A failure of an assignment tends to be seen more as a miscalculation on the part of the therapist rather than resistance on the part of the client/family.

Directives

Brief/strategic approaches are often directive in that a client or family will be given ideas or even instructions on how to behave in particular situations. Sometimes directives will require specific changes in behaviors, sometimes they will require that changes be avoided or delayed. Therapists concerned with process tend to focus on directives to be carried out between sessions, using the interview to gather information and to develop the kind of rapport necessary for a respectful, cooperative relationship. Therapists concerned with form also give directives for between sessions but will often direct families to do something different during interviews. For example, a parent might be directed to control a disruptive child there and then, while the therapist blocks any attempts by a grandparent or the parentified child to intrude. The session is used to rehearse changes that the family may be directed to carry out at home. Such sessions can sometimes become very dramatic.

Madanes observes:

> The approach assumes that all therapy is directive and that a therapist cannot avoid being directive, since even the issues he chooses to comment on and his tone of voice are directive. (1981b, p. 23)

The therapist must therefore become skilled at influencing people and maximizing the likelihood of directives being accepted or carried out. Cade has noted:

Typically, strategic therapists do not see motivation simply as either existing or not existing within the family members. Motivation is seen as a function of the interchange between family and therapist. Lack of motivation will be more usefully looked at as a response to the therapist's response to the family. (1980b, p. 95)

It is also important to consider how to respond to the way people deal with directives. Have they been followed, modified, opposed, ignored, or forgotten? The therapist must be guided by such feedback in order to determine the next step. For example, if directives are followed as requested, then further such directives may be indicated; if opposed, then "paradoxical" directives might be indicated. If directives are forgotten or ignored, then the therapist must carefully consider his or her position. Often the therapist will have become more motivated for change than the client or family, and should be prepared to adopt a more cautious and respectful one-down position.

Also typical of most brief/strategic therapists is the belief that, in terms of the meanings that can be attributed to events, no absolute reality exists, only constructs (Kelly, 1955) or "mental maps" through which people make sense of their experiences and which govern their reactions and responses to, and their thinking about, those experiences. They operate from the assumption that if the way that the world is viewed can be questioned and modified, then meaning can be changed, and thus also the experiential and the behavioral consequences of meaning. This belief has led to the importance of the use of reframing and relabeling.

Brief/strategic therapists also make considerable use of the art of communicating through analogy. Anecdotes, parables, stories, and humor can be used to facilitate the process of therapy. These aspects will be looked at in more detail in later chapters, as will the recent development of the future/solution-focused approaches, which build on what people are already doing that is working for them (Berg & Miller, 1992; de Shazer,

1985, 1988; de Shazer et al., 1986; Dolan, 1991; Furman & Ahola, 1992; O'Hanlon & Martin, 1992; O'Hanlon & Weiner-Davis, 1989; Walter & Peller, 1992; White & Epston, 1990).

TRAINING

The basic theoretical underpinnings of the brief/strategic approaches are relatively easy to learn, as are many of the basic interviewing skills. However, the respectful, creative, effective use of the approach is extremely difficult to learn (taking a substantial part of the rest of a therapist's life).

Haley outlines several criteria for selection and training.

1. He suggests that, as the approach "stresses problems in the real world, it is best to choose students with experience of that world." He favors the selection of mature students with children, rather than young people.
2. The student should have both intelligence and a wide range of behaviors—the ability to be "authoritarian, at times playful, at times flirtatious, at times grim and serious, at times helpless, and so on."
3. The learning of several approaches concurrently should be avoided.
4. Ideally, the student should learn by doing therapy and being guided right from the start by an experienced supervisor using live supervision techniques. The role-play of specific techniques can be useful before trying them out on a client/family.
5. Learning in groups maximizes learning opportunities by increasing the number of cases seen, the range of ideas available and by offering peer support.
6. The accent should be on practice rather than on theory; watching and showing therapy sessions rather than discussing therapy.
7. The training should be focused on what to do with the issues arising in the student's current work. Thus the student remains highly motivated to learn.
8. The supervisor must teach the student how to be directive

and how to motivate people. (It is our view, paradoxically, that it is also important to learn how to be directive in order to be able effectively to choose in any particular case to be non-directive.)

9. Therapy should be oriented towards problems and solutions rather than methods, and cases should be selected where possible to give learning opportunities in specific areas where individual students are encountering difficulties.

10. Students should be required to check the outcome of their work and to learn follow-up procedures.

11. Training should take place in a context supportive of the approach and the style of training, as well as having the appropriate technical equipment such as one-way screens and videotaping and/or audiotaping facilities. (Haley, 1976, pp. 179–194)

CONCLUSION

The field of brief/strategic therapy has been expanding rapidly and techniques proliferating such that it is almost impossible to do justice to its richness and diversity. This overview has sought to identify the main themes and developments.

Brief/strategic approaches appear to have an extremely wide applicability. Madanes notes that "Since in strategic therapy a specific therapeutic plan is designed for each problem, there are no contra-indications in terms of patient selection and suitability"(Madanes, 1981b, p. 27). Stanton lists a vast range of problems that have effectively been treated using these approaches, from straightforward behavioral problems, delinquency, marital problems to more serious neurotic and psychotic problems (1981, pp. 368–69). He argues that "strategic therapists are less likely to reject particular kinds of problem families than they are to shun situations where the context of the situation permits little or no leverage" (p. 369).

Stanton claims that "investigators of strategic therapy have been more active than researchers in other family therapy approaches as far as performing controlled or comparative family therapy outcome research is concerned" (p. 396). He draws particular attention to the work of Parsons and Alexander in which a strategic approach was compared to three other approaches to treating delinquency and demonstrated to be markedly more effective (Parsons & Alexander, 1973).

To end this chapter on a more cautionary note, many young, newly-trained therapists are attracted to the excitement and promise of the brief/strategic approaches and by the "wizardry" demonstrated at workshops or in the literature. Also, as Greenberg points out, "the assumption is made that because the therapy is brief it is simple to carry out." He continues:

> Therapists new to the format often familiarize themselves with the literature then hurriedly attempt to apply brief principles and techniques without the particular information needed for assessment and treatment. Also, the novice team tends to attempt "cookbook interventions" that are primarily based on descriptions from the literature. . . . (Greenberg, 1980, p. 320)

Beginners will often overconcentrate on technique, on devising "clever" interventions, paying insufficient attention to respect, understanding, and validation. This may be, to some extent, the fault of writers on brief/strategic approaches, including ourselves, who may at times have overconcentrated on techniques and interventions and underplayed the importance of basic attitudes and values, and of wisdom, integrity, and restraint, having taken it for granted that these qualities were already valued by the reader. Brief/strategic therapists have also not been very good at demonstrating the patient, painstaking, and sometimes exhaustive groundwork that often precedes the "brilliant" interventions, nor the many cases in which steady, competent work rather than dramatic "fireworks" has brought about significant changes. Wisdom does not develop overnight nor can it be learned at a workshop, however well presented. It develops over years of rigorous trial and error.

2

WHAT IS IT THAT HAPPENS BETWEEN THE EARS?

A universe comes into being when a space is severed or taken apart. The skin of a living organism cuts off an outside from an inside. So does the circumference of a circle in a plane. By tracing the way we represent such a severance, we can begin to reconstruct, with an accuracy and coverage that appear almost uncanny, the basic forms underlying linguistic, mathematical, physical, and biological science, and can begin to see how the familiar laws of our own experience follow inexorably from the original act of severance.

—Spencer-Brown (1979, p. xxix)

. . . none of our explanations can be true . . . in some sense there is no ultimate truth accessible to us for the simple reason we have to make a cut in the Universe in order to do the experiment at all. We have to decide what is relevant and what is irrelevant.

—Bronowski (1978, p. 69)

. . . without his inventions, both theoretical and instrumental, man would be both disorientated and blind. He would not know where to look or how to see.

—Kelly (1969, p. 94)

The deepest feeling of all is that there should be more.

—Harrison (1986, p. 2)

There has been increasing concern expressed in recent years that brief therapists typically show little interest in what it is that happens between the ears. The "black box" analogy has been criticized as ignoring clients' felt experiences, a significant motivating factor in how they respond to their world, and a crucial component in their ongoing sense of self (Duncan, 1992). Brief therapists are certainly usually more concerned with observable phenomena. We are essentially in agreement with the importance of focusing on the observable and of minimizing the number of inferences and assumptions made when attempting to understand human behavior. However, we do have brains and something quite clearly does go on inside them. While making the minimum of assumptions, we want briefly to present some related frameworks (at least, related in our minds). We have found these helpful in considering how people make sense of their world and discriminate for themselves the unique "realities" within which each lives and responds, both *behaviorally* and *affectively*.

THE BASIC OPERATION

The basic building block of all life other than at the most primitive level (amoebae, certain politicians, etc.) is the nerve cell, which operates strictly on an "all or nothing" principle: It either fires or it does not fire; a most basic distinction, ON or OFF. Each cell's decision to transmit will be based on its particular and unchanging threshold level of excitability, and it can never transmit extra levels of information in any other way (for example, by any variation in its intensity of response) other than in the frequency with which it fires. The process of evolution to higher forms of functioning is based primarily on the gradual building up of increasingly rich and varied ways of "wiring up" synaptic connections between increasing numbers of these basic nerve cells, each one of which remains able only to indicate one of two potential states.

Spencer-Brown proposed the most basic of operations to be the drawing of a distinction which, once drawn, creates two spaces or states, separated by a boundary, either space or state capable of being marked (named) (Spencer-Brown, 1979, p. 1). That this operation is being performed implies that there must first exist a distinction between observer and the field of observation. Whatever it is that produces the impetus, at any point, for a distinction to be drawn will determine which side of a boundary becomes the more significant such that the other becomes that which is not the former.

Quite clearly, the more primitive a form of life, the fewer will be the distinctions that need to be drawn in order that it be able to function within the parameters defined by its form: distinctions, for example, between hot and not-hot, cold and not-cold, dark and not-dark, light and not-light, wet and not-wet, dry and not-dry, edible and not-edible, safe and not-safe, dangerous and not-dangerous, etc. The more complex the life form, the greater the number and variety of distinctions it will be capable of drawing. The more complex the sensory apparatus and nervous system, the more subtle and varied will be the distinctions that the life form is capable of drawing.

Clearly it is possible to draw distinctions within distinctions. For example, an organism's response to drawing a distinction between edible and not-edible will be affected by the distinction it draws between near and not-near, tired and not-tired, or hungry and not-hungry. Distinctions that define the degree of urgency and intensity with which other distinctions are viewed can lead to them being organized into a variety of hierarchical arrangements. For example, an intense feeling of hunger might prompt a tired animal to pursue something that is not-near but edible. Alternatively, intense tiredness may lead to a hungry animal ignoring something edible but not-near. Something near and edible might evoke no response from an animal that is not tired but also not hungry. These are somewhat oversimplified examples, but already it can be seen that, even when a minimal range of distinctions can be drawn, a considerable degree of complexity in an organism's experience of and responses to its environment becomes possible.

The size and ability of the human brain, the complexity of our sensory apparatus and our nervous system, and our capacity for abstract thinking, means that the range and complexity of hierarchies of distinctions that we can draw effectively becomes infinite.

In spite of attempts of sociobiologists to explain as much as possible of our behavior as genetically determined, it seems that we can reliably be seen to be "wired up" in respect of only a relatively few rather basic traits. We appear genetically to be driven to eat, to defend ourselves, or to flee when necessary, to gather into social groupings, to reproduce, and to care for our offspring. We also appear disposed to laugh, often in relation to the exercise of our almost insatiable curiosity about the nature of our surrounding with its endless supply of puzzles. In this, we are not very different from chimpanzees, who can be described in largely the same way. What is different is that, with our larger brains, we are also, according to Chomsky, "wired up" for symbolic language development, and it is through language that we have been able to realize and articulate a multitude of worlds ranging from the most basic and practical to the most abstract and metaphysical (Chomsky, 1972, 1975).

It is through the richness of symbolic language that the distinctions we draw and the meanings we confer are articulated, interpreted, and reinterpreted in the continued evolutionary process of constructing our "realities." We do this through the medium of internal and interpersonal dialogues. As Goolishian and Anderson observe:

> In the hermeneutic sense, humans construct the worlds they do because they participate in language, in social practices, in institutions, and in other forms of symbolic action. These social actions presuppose, demand, and warrant the very constructions of the world and self which are current to that participation. (1992, p. 11)

PERSONAL CONSTRUCTS

Psychologist George Kelly proposed a framework for understanding human behavior based primarily on the drawing of distinctions (Kelly, 1955). This framework appears, in our view, to postulate a basic process similar to Spencer-Brown's "most basic operation," as well as adhering to William of Occam's principle of parsimony in hypothesizing. Describing Kelly's contribution to the various theories of personality, Schultz comments:

> Kelly's theory shares little with the other approaches. He warned us that we will not find in his system many of the familiar terms and concepts commonly found in personality theories. Having warned us, he then proceeded to shock us by pointing out how many of these terms are missing in his approach: unconscious, need, drive, stimulus, response, reinforcement, and — most amazing of all — motivation and emotion. (1990, p. 380)

The essential postulate in Kelly's theory is that situations are made sense of through the application of a variety of "constructs," which make up the unique way each of us draws distinctions and categorizes our experiences, thus affecting the ways in which we anticipate future events. Over time, all of us develop a variety of dimensions, or sets of categories, that are of particular importance to us in analyzing and responding to the world. These reflect all of our varied experiences to date (as we currently remember and interpret them) and our present principle concerns. These not only affect our perceptions of and responses to current situations, but also our anticipation of, and preparations for, how the future is likely to be. Constructs exist primarily in the eye of the beholder and should therefore not be considered as entities that actually exist. They are interpretations of, rather than reflections of, objective reality. They are continually subject to revision. We will consider in Chapter 3 some of the problems that can arise when abstractions become treated as though they were concrete entities. All personal perception is highly selective and individual (although people of the same family, ethnic background, religious faith, political persuasion, gender, etc., can, of course, share many constructs, confirming them through continued rituals and dialogue).

Constructs can be elicited, for example, by asking a subject to select a list of ten to fifteen people in different kinds of significant relationships (e.g., father, mother, sibling, teacher, priest, friend, lover, foreigner) or, alternatively, the list can be supplied by the experimenter. Then, taking three from the list at a time, he or she is asked to say which two of the selected three are most similar and the way in which the other one differs. After a while, as different combinations are selected, a list of preferred characteristics can begin to be identified. A grid can be made up demonstrating the dimensions along which the subject tends to make distinctions when assessing people. Argyle points out that, "Different people use different traits. . . . People become most accurate in assessing whatever qualities concern them most . . . " (Argyle, 1983, p. 107).

Fransella and Bannister explain a construct as a discrimination, not a verbal label.

> Kelly offers several definitions of a construct. For example, a construct is "a way in which two or more things are alike and *thereby* different from a third or more things." . . . In all his definitions, Kelly retains the essential notion that constructs are bipolar. His argument is that we never affirm anything without simultaneously denying something. . . . We do not always, or even very often, specify our contrast pole, but Kelly's argument is that we make sense out of our world by simultaneously noting likenesses *and* differences. It is in the contrast that the usefulness of the construct subsists. (1977, p. 5)

Although scientists are not yet sure how memory is stored, it seems clear that the process involves the storage of patterns of association between sensory impulses. It is this storage of patterns, rather than a sequential storing of each individual sensory event, which enables us to operate on limited amounts of information. Access to a part of a pattern allows an almost instantaneous appreciation of a way to complete the pattern based on previously learned associations, on the mapping of incoming data onto patterns stored in the memory. (It is easy to see the evolutionary advantages accruing from the ability thus to respond.)

Peter Russell (1979) has suggested that "information is recorded in vast interconnecting networks. Each idea or image has hundreds, perhaps thousands of associations and is connected to numerous other points in the mental network" (1979, p. 105).

Pathways between associations that are more frequently repeated tend to become reinforced. Those less frequently used, though not erased, probably tend to become less important or "forgotten" in the same way that unused pathways through a forest will become overgrown and forgotten unless reopened through subsequent use.

As patterns of associations become established so they will tend to influence the selection and flow of subsequent information. As de Bono has suggested, "patterns are picked out of the environment solely on the basis of familiarity, and through such selection become ever more familiar" (1971, p. 124). In this way, we develop hierarchies of patterns of distinctions within distinctions that will tend to govern how we see ourselves, our world, and how we ascribe meaning to our experiences. We will define the structures we create from these abstractions as "reality." Clearly, of prime importance are those distinctions that need to be drawn to preserve life and safety. The drawing of distinctions can be based on constructs that are relatively easily articulated and available to introspection, through those distinctions that reflect more deeply buried memories of experiences and conditionings, down to the level of our most basic and less articulatable instincts. Again, how these become hierarchically organized at any time can depend on context. Faced with a child at risk, an adult may, without thinking (or regardless of that thinking), face something about which, in a different context, he or she might be either irrationally phobic or reasonably terrified.

Other important dimensions for drawing distinctions are those through which we define various categories of *them* and *us*, for example, family, tribe, race, gender, color, religious belief, class, and the myriad of other groupings that can assume either a profound and longlasting or a transitory importance in our lives.

once events are assigned into a global category, further observations about them tend to be biased . . . tend to be assigned
to behaviors even on the basis of little information. . . . After global labels are applied they may become difficult to dis-
confirm and to discard. Moreover, if broad trait categories are
widely shared and commonly used in a culture, they may come
to seem like intuitively appropriate descriptions for behaviors
that they actually do not fit well.

It often has been found that after an individual categorizes
or groups stimuli he tends to retain his category even in the
face of contradictory evidence, paying less attention to the new
information and focusing instead on information that confirms
his category. (Mischel, 1968, p. 58)

Sometimes, only a few primary dimensions predominate.
Many other potential dimensions can thus collapse into those
few that are seen as the more inclusive, and a rigidity of attitude and response can develop over a brief or a more prolonged
period. For example, dimensions such as goodness or badness,
status, intelligence, attractiveness, can be considerably affected when construed through the lenses of hierarchically
more superior (to us) dimensions such as family, tribe, color,
religion, looking "just like his uncle Jack," etc. At a far more
trivial level, the distinctions commonly drawn between those
with red hair and the rest of us can affect our attitude toward
and tolerance of outbursts of fiery anger. When under pressure
(and what is experienced as pressure is, to some considerable
extent, in the eye of the beholder), any of us is likely to narrow
our focus down to those dimensions that seem the most important for immediate survival. Certain extreme political or religious fundamentalist positions can act as "black holes" into
which veritable universes of dimensions can permanently disappear under the imperatives of a few dominant themes. As
de Bono observes:

A particular danger that arises from the tendency to treat
things in terms of opposite poles is that the poles become as
far apart as possible. . . . So any distinction at all is magnified
into an absolute distinction. Exactly the same effect accounts

for the process in which a partial description takes over as a total description. A politician is easily labeled as corrupt, a woman as a bitch, even though only a small part of their behavior justifies this description. But if this small part is the only part that is distinctive then it is taken as representative of the whole. (1971, pp. 201–2)

Schultz points out that constructs can range from being permeable such that they are "capable of being revised and extended in the light of new experiences," to those that appear impermeable such that they seem "not capable of being revised or replaced, no matter what new experiences are available. . . . A person can tolerate a number of subordinate inconsistencies without discarding or modifying the overall construct" (Schultz, 1990, pp. 390–1). Thus, cognitive complexity, which may be defined in terms of the larger number of independent dimensions available to be used in the drawing of distinctions at any time, can arguably be equated with flexibility, responsiveness, tolerance, understanding, creativity, etc. There will presumably be a whole complex of personal, interpersonal, group membership (including race and gender), historical, and sociopolitical factors that will affect the relative constancy or otherwise in each of us of any particular cluster of related constructs.

FIGURE/GROUND:
THE EFFECTS OF OBSERVER BIAS

Thus, in any field toward which our attention is drawn, certain aspects of the situation will stand out in a figure/ground relation to other aspects. A friend of one of us, many years ago, bought a Victorian drawing which was a rather skillfully executed reversible figure/ground picture of the type frequently used in works on the psychology of perception. The picture could be seen either as a naked young woman or as a collection of gaunt human skulls. The friend had only seen the former figure and was unable to see the latter until some time after it was pointed out. He was looking absentmindedly at it several days later when suddenly he was able to see the skulls for the first time. Clearly, in such a drawing, the emergence of either subject depends on two totally different interpretations of which lines and which areas of shade constitute the figure against which all of the rest then goes to make up the ground. The two subjects cannot exist simultaneously for any one observer (although they can rapidly be alternated between, once you have developed the hang of it). Discussing the figure/ground phenomenon in a chapter on perception, Adcock comments that "detail is observable in the portion regarded as figure whereas the background tends to be rather homogenous" (1964, p. 142).

As was demonstrated by the studies of Robert Rosenthal and his colleagues on the effects of experimenter bias, the sense we make of things, what we choose as figure and what we choose as ground, and our predictions about the future not only affect our own behaviors, they can profoundly affect the behaviors of others (Rosenthal, 1966; Rosenthal & Jacobson, 1968). In one of their experiments, a group of teachers were informed that all of the children in their classes had been given an intelligence test to predict which of them were likely to blossom. They were given the names of those who were alleged to have scored highly in this test. For each class, the "special children" had actually been chosen randomly. Thus, the differences between the "special children" and the rest existed solely in the minds of the teachers. It was found that, after one year

> a significant expectancy advantage was found, and it was especially great among children of the first and second grades. The advantage of having been expected to bloom was evident for these younger children in total IQ, verbal IQ, and reasoning IQ. The control group of children of these grades gained well in IQ, 19 percent of them gaining twenty or more total IQ points. The "special" children, however, showed 47 percent of their number gaining twenty or more total IQ points. (Rosenthal & Jacobson, 1968, p. 175)

Other researchers have highlighted the effects of our expectations not only on the way that things are viewed but on the serious implications of the actions that can stem from the way distinctions thus become drawn. Rosenhan reported on the research that persuasively demonstrated the impossibility of reliably distinguishing between the sane and the insane in psychiatric hospitals, where a reality is constructed such that any behavior, however normal, can come to be seen as a self-evident sign of insanity. On the file of one of the pseudo-patient/researchers, who had openly made extensive written notes about his experience, appeared the comment "Patient engages in writing behavior." He had apparently never been asked by any staff member what it was he was writing down (Rosenhan, 1973).

As one of us has said elsewhere:

> As our patterns of association become established in a particular way, they will tend to influence the processing of subsequent experiences. . . . In this way we develop belief frameworks or mental "sets" that determine how we see ourselves and our world, and how we ascribe meaning, and thus respond to, those experiences. In our relationships with others, we then develop patterns of behaving together that both reflect our mental sets and those of the people with whom we interact, and tend by repetition to be confirmed – though such patterns rarely develop consciously. (Cade, 1991, p. 35)

This process has been succinctly described by Zukav:

> Reality is what we take to be true. What we take to be true is what we believe. What we believe is based upon our perceptions. What we perceive depends upon what we look for. What we look for depends upon what we think. What we think depends upon what we perceive. What we perceive determines what we believe. What we believe determines what we take to be true. What we take to be true is our reality. (1979, p. 328)

We are not arguing that the above represent the truth about what happens between the ears. They represent the most parsimonious frameworks for understanding mental processes based on the basic operation of our basic building blocks and in which the fewest possible assumptions are made.

3

THE REALITY OF "REALITY" (OR THE "REALITY" OF REALITY): "WHAT IS REALLY HAPPENING?"

*... reasoning about causes and effects is a very difficult thing.
... We are already hard put to establish a relationship between
such an obvious effect as a charred tree and the lightning bolt
that set fire to it, so to trace sometimes endless chains of causes
and effects seems to me as foolish as trying to build a tower that
will touch the sky.*

—The Name of the Rose, *Eco (1983)*

Some recent works have begun a debate in our field about the nature of reality. Watzlawick (1984) edited a book entitled *The Invented Reality* in which a number of contributors argued variously that reality is no more than a construction, an invention, arising out of the way each observer views the world. Speed, on the other hand, argued what she calls a co-constructivist position: Reality does exist and our constructions are a more or less adequate reflection of that reality and are in an interpenetrating relationship with it (1984a, 1984b, 1991).

Here we will seek to highlight some problems in this debate that can arise, in our opinion, from a failure to differentiate clearly between two levels: (1) the level of things and events, and (2) the meanings placed upon them. We will also argue an anarchistic position that, on the one hand, even if there were an absolute reality, it would be best not to believe in it, and, on the other hand, any view of reality, however apparently absurd, might be worth believing in at some time or other. In other words, we should believe in nothing and everything, both at the same time. To do any less can lead to the many absurd positions that we see taken around us in our seemingly crazy and suicidal world.

THINGS and EVENTS are limited to sensory-based observations and descriptions of what we perceive, or remember perceiving, through our various senses; what is happening, or has happened.

MEANINGS are interpretations, conclusions, beliefs, and attributions that are derived from, imposed upon, or related to these perceived things and events.

Let us start it off with the level of reality that involves things and events. It seems to us sensible that we accept for ourselves, for most purposes, such a level of reality. Generally (though this may not necessarily be so with other life-forms yet to be discovered), all will agree essentially on the existence and dimensions of particular things and that changes occur within and between things over particular timescales that can be both observed and measured by us. It is in the interpretation of and the ascription of meaning to those things and events that differences, sometimes dramatic and far-reaching, occur.

This was nicely highlighted in Scheflen's paper "Susan Smiled: On Explanation in Family Therapy" (1978). Doubtless all observers of the event mentioned in the title of that paper would agree, given time for analysis, that Susan's lips moved in a certain way at a particular point and in relation chronologically to the behaviors of the other people in the room. However, it was in the selection and highlighting of what things and events were significant and in the ascription of meaning to these that the observers differed. In the discussion group described in the article, such differences in interpretation seemed to lead to little more than an interesting and prolonged discussion on the possible meanings of Susan's smile. In other contexts, this same phenomenon, that things and events can be viewed in many and sometimes conflicting ways, can lead to the development of a whole range of human problems spanning from relatively minor squabbles up to religious persecution, major wars, and who knows, perhaps even to total global annihilation.

It must, at this point, be admitted that, once we move down in scale to subatomic levels, we immediately hit upon problems with definitions of reality. However solid a piece of rock may seem to be when experienced through the unaided human senses, when probed at the subatomic level it becomes rather insubstantial and elusive. It appears to be formed of relationships between miniscule particles that exist briefly in a world of probabilities (and which may only be brought into existence by the actual process of observation). As Capra observes, "the concept of matter in sub-atomic physics . . . is totally different from the traditional idea of a material substance in classical physics. The same is true for concepts like space, time, or cause and effect" (1976, p. 15). Or, as physicist Henry Pierce Stapp proposes in an unpublished paper, quoted in Zukav's fascinating work, *The Dancing Wu-Li Masters*:

> If the attitude of quantum mechanics is correct, in the strong sense that a description of the substructure underlying experience more complete than the one it provides is not possible, then there is no substantive physical world, in the usual sense of the term. The conclusion here is not the weak conclusion that there *may* not be a substantive physical world but rather that there definitely is not a substantive physical world. (1979, p. 105)

For our purposes, however, we will remain somewhat above the subatomic level, at a level on which the things and events we experience in our environment can reasonably be taken as "out there."

Watzlawick seems, at times, to take a somewhat extreme position; to argue that there is no "out there" reality but only that which is, in the "most immediate and concrete sense" (1984, p. 10), constructed by the observer. By not differentiating clearly between levels, between things and events and the meanings that can be ascribed to them, he seems to be taking an almost solipsistic position, one that it would be interesting to invite him to elaborate further whilst standing in front of an irate polar bear. Is the creature "really" there? However, a discussion among a fur trader, an Eskimo, a big-game hunter seeking trophies, and an environmentalist, might well demonstrate that, though none of them would argue about the reality of such creatures existing, they might differ radically in the way they viewed them and thus treated them.

Of course, as Rosenthal demonstrated, the beliefs and expectations of an observer can have a direct and self-fulfilling influence on the behavior of people or creatures under observation (as also seems to be the case with subatomic particles) (Rosenthal, 1966). Selection of perceptions according to bias leads to particular responses from the observer that transmit information tending to influence towards and reinforce certain behaviors in those under observation in line with the expectations of the observer, and usually largely outside of the conscious awareness of either party. Therefore, an observer's attitude toward polar bears may well influence how the creature behaves toward him or her, therefore "constructing" an aspect of reality. Yet the physical polar bear still exists separate to the process of observation (or if it doesn't in any absolute sense, on the level of physical reality that we all inhabit it would be wise to believe that this is so).

Speed, on the other hand, errs toward another extreme. Again, by failing to differentiate clearly between the different levels she seems to be equating, for example, the clearly definable physical structure of a mountain with some equally absolute and definable "reality" or "truth" about what is happening in a family, towards which, by increasingly refining models, the observer can get closer and closer. She proposes that a hypothesis about a family is useful because it is "true" (or rather, as she goes on to correct herself, because "it is a relatively more adequate reflection or model of reality").

A family's "reality" is a somewhat complex thing. At one

level most observers would agree on the number of participants, their sex, size, and other facets of appearance, and on
the events that occur between the various members (e.g.,
mother turns around 180 degrees, raises her voice several deci-
bels, speaks a certain number of words; father, on the fourth
word, turns quickly 170 degrees around and walks out of the
door; as father reaches a point two meters from the door, tears
appear in the daughter's eyes; the mother moves across and
puts her left arm around her daughter's shoulder, etc. Such
analyses can be made at a microscopic level, split second by
split second, or at a less detailed level over longer time spans).
However, when it comes to applying meanings to the events,
things become much more complex:

> In any given situation there are potentially limitless facets of
> the total gestalt of externally and internally derived experi-
> ences that can serve to recreate the original conditions that
> can cause a whole range of memories and associations to be
> "recovered." Which of these facets of experience become high-
> lighted at any particular time against the huge backdrop of
> potential associations depends on the particular conscious or
> less conscious concerns occupying us at that point in time.
> . . . In other words, our particular concerns, the particular fo-
> cuses derived from our frameworks for applying meaning, will
> through intensification separate out certain features or aspects
> of experience from the implicit or potential richness of associa-
> tions possible. As patterns of association become established
> in a particular way, so they will tend to influence the processing
> of subsequent experiences. (Cade, 1991, p. 35)

In any event or series of events involving several people,
the situation will be infinitely more complex; a complicated
web of distinctions drawn, memories, associations, and relationships between each participant's processes of selection and
patterning, influenced by individual, family, cultural, religious, racial, and national myths about what is and what has
been, what should or could have been, and what ought to be,
observable only through a similar process on the part of the
observer.

An oversimplified example – a man may, through a whole

complex of conditionings, experiences, prejudices, myths, etc., have developed the idea that certain women (or all women) cannot be trusted and that they are always trying to control men through female wiles and underhand schemes. He will tend to perceive (and react to, accordingly) the actions of any woman with whom he is involved through this set of beliefs. Let us assume that, in an earlier relationship, this man had come, through constructs stemming probably from a complex of both his personal and societal "conditionings," to see the woman in that earlier relationship as "pursuing" and trying to "entrap" such that he eventually reacted (from his perspective) accordingly.

A woman who has, in her turn, developed the idea that certain men (or all men) cannot commit themselves emotionally and are always attempting to dominate and control as though they have the right to do so, will also tend to perceive (and react accordingly to) the actions of any man with whom she is involved in this light. If this couple were to make a relationship, their interactional pattern will develop from these reactions and counterreactions (which will partly, even largely, have their genesis in the "constructs" of preceding generations as well as in those of the prevailing societal norms). It is through the constructs (or internal dialogues), through which each of us views and "makes sense of" what is happening in any relationship or set of relationships (regardless of whether we are right or wrong, assuming that this can ever reliably be ascertained), that we decide how to act.

For a while, the man may experience this woman differently than the woman in his earlier relationship and thus act differently. However, it may be that, if this relationship were to proceed for any length of time, his general beliefs about how women behave in long-term relationships might begin to affect how he interprets certain of her behaviors such that he could start to detect "pursuit" and "entrapment" and begin withdrawing and thus invite just that range of behaviors from her that he most fears. In her turn, though initially she may experience him differently, the woman's general belief that "most men become emotionally distant" could lead her to anticipate and thus to interpret aspects of his subsequent behaviors as evidence of the first signs of withdrawal such that her fears are aroused, leading her to "pursue" such that she invites just the range of behaviors from him that *she* most fears.

We act in accordance with the motives and agendas we attribute to, and thus use to explain, the actions of others (rightly or wrongly) as well as in accordance with our own agendas (which we might be more or less aware of at any one time). People inadvertently ensnare each other in "games" (sometimes tragic in their consequences) as they attempt both to promote and to protect their interests (which might equally include the interests of others, however misguidedly perceived or represented these may be).

This will, of course, also be true of how we experience the actions of our partners in their relations with our children (as well as the actions of all their, and our, involved relatives), and also our children's actions in their relations both with us and with our spouses (and all those other relatives).

There will be a multitude of factors influencing how we interpret these actions. These will include aspects of how our family and marital relationships have developed (in *our* view), personal conditionings and injunctions (i.e., through our own family experiences) about the nature of marriage and what one can expect from it, and about the place of children, of each sex, in the marital relationship, as well as societal imperatives and stereotypes about these. We will then react in accordance with the motives and agendas we attribute to these actions, which can include, for example, the attribution by us of "dirty" motives on the part of the spouse or the child, or both, and on the part of others (Palazzoli et al., 1989), as well as our own motives and agendas. The power of the "Pygmalion effect," the self-fulfilling prophecy, then comes into play.

In their turn, children will pick up beliefs about themselves (also from family as well as societal values and attitudes), including, in families with chronic problems, the possibility of many self-denigrating ideas. Among these beliefs (which we see as "existing" in a complex hierarchy of interlocking themes) will exist ideas about the roles they must adopt in relation to parents and siblings, the wider family and society, such as "savior," "angel," "ally," "favorite," "villain,"

"persecutor," "victim," "success," "failure," etc. The more you
behave towards somebody as though they *are* a particular
way, the more likely they are to *become* that way. The more
you behave as though you, yourself, *are* a particular way, the
more you are likely to *become* that way.

All that needs then to be added to the brew is for *more of
the same* pattern to be repeatedly acted out and intensified,
influenced continually by the application of *more of the same*
ways of construing what is going on, leading to *more of the
same* attributions being made about the actions of the other
participants in the game, and so on.

Implicit in Speed's position seems to be a belief in concrete
patterns or structures that exist in a family and in its internal
and external relationships and also in a hidden yet explicit
structure to the individual and shared unconscious processes
which select and pattern experiences and out of which the participants respond and react to each other.

Welwood suggests:

> the traditional model of the unconscious in depth psychology
> makes it appear as though the unconscious has an explicit
> structure to it, as though drives, wishes, repressions, or arche-
> types exist in an explicit form, as though the unconscious were
> a kind of autonomous alter-ego. . . . What is unconscious are
> holistic patternings, which may be explicated in many different
> ways and at many different levels of the organism/environment
> interrelationship. (1982, p. 133)

In the realm of meaning attribution, the fact that a map or
model or belief framework is adequate does not thus mean in
any absolute sense that it is somehow true or nearer to an
absolute "truth" than some other adequate model. All that can
be said is that the patterns of associations selected, the connections made and the meanings attributed (or perhaps it might
be more accurate to say "imposed"), through the medium of
such frameworks, are more or less useful or functional having
regard to purpose (i.e., are useful for explanation and prediction). Speed refers to "the reality of the family's patterns"; here,
she makes a fundamental error by confusing levels of reality.
Patterns are connections between elements, between things

and events, that are drawn by an observer. Of course, the things and events can be taken, for most purposes, to exist "out there," but the patterns belong at a different level and are imposed by the observer, arising from particular frameworks for drawing distinctions, and developing understanding, relating to particular purposes on his or her part.

Figure 1 should clarify this. At the top of the diagram are drawn 24 dots (which can be accepted by the reader, for the purposes of this chapter, as really existing "out there"). The rest of the page is taken up with but a few of the more straightforward of the patterns that can be "imposed" as a way of drawing and highlighting the relationship between the dots, commencing with their being seen as four horizontal rows of six dots, then six vertical rows of four dots, and so on.

Speed's position would assume that all these patterns, together presumably with the countless others possible (and we haven't started using curved lines yet), are *really* there in the dots, unrelated to the act of observing. Here she falls prey to what A. N. Whitehead called "The Fallacy of Misplaced Concreteness." As Waddington explains:

> Most conventional thought . . . recognises certain derived, and essentially abstract, notions, that have been invented by man to try to make sense of the situations he comes across. Examples are physical atoms, or feelings such as anger, or social notions such as justice. Man tends to accept these notions as being concrete things, which could, as it were, be picked up and placed somewhere else. Whitehead argued that such notions are in fact always derived from actual occasions of human experience. The experiences are the real things; the notions are secondary and derivative. It is dangerous to forget this, and to take these secondary things as more concrete and real than they actually are. (1977, p. 24)

Obviously, in any explanatory framework, there must be a significant degree of "fit" between the two levels ("significant" being that level of "fit" necessary for the observer to be able to explain and predict sufficient to his or her purposes). Just as the patterns in the diagram must fit the number and spatial

FIGURE 1

distribution of the dots, so, with a family, a therapist's ideas about what is happening must fit, at one level, with the people involved and with sufficient "significant" events that occur (as well as with the participants' ideas about these matters). Even with that constraint, as with the dots, there is an immense variety of patterns and explanations that can be "imposed" by an observer (probably as many as there are observers available) though, of course, familial, gender, cultural, educational, professional, theoretical, and many other influences in common between observers will mean that there may be considerable convergence in respect of many facets.

We would argue that the realities we construct that help us devise helpful interactions or interventions do so because of a sufficient fit with significant (to them) facets of family members' constructed realities, their ways of thinking about themselves. A family's "reality" will be but one way of making sense of, and responding both behaviorally and affectively to, the things and events they experience (real, to them) among the many available. The therapist's skill lies in finding a way of viewing a family's reality that is near enough to its members' views to engage it, albeit briefly, in a "shared reality," yet with sufficiently different perspectives to help bring about the development of changes in meanings and thus in experience and in response. Getting close to a family's "reality" no more means that a therapist has found *the* reality than guessing which pattern a family uses as a way of organizing the 24 dots in the diagram means that that pattern is thus the real pattern. All the other patterns can fit equally well.

The Buddha has offered advice to seekers after truth; to regard the world of material objects, emotions, relationships, etc., as "reality," is to live in error, just as much as to regard all as merely illusion is to live in just as big an error.

It is my contention that all human problems, at all levels of functioning from the individual up to the international, arise out of the reification of belief frameworks, of views of reality, and from the repeated patterns of response that evolve out of those frameworks. (This statement, of course, refers also to

itself and should not be treated too respectfully.) To be therapeutic it is thus important, it seems to me, that we become
anarchistic in our approaches, that we believe nothing, and
everything, both at the same time! Whenever our therapy becomes informed by diagnostic and therapeutic orthodoxy, by
strongly held personal beliefs, then we impose and delimit, we
encourage, and in some circumstances attempt to enforce, orthodoxy in thought and action (sometimes in the name of its
opposite). (Cade, 1985a, p. 10)

Yet, in order to consider anything we have to have a framework for thinking about it. The error is not that we have frameworks but that we forget that they are only frameworks and
confuse them with reality. Once we take a position on anything
we begin to close our minds to other possibilities and then
tend to select and interpret data that confirms that position
and to not see, ignore, or reject what contradicts it. This is
a process one of us has called "hardening of the categories"
(O'Hanlon, 1990). This is, of course, not a problem where it is
not a problem but, when problems do develop, this can become
a major problem. Then the phenomenon that Rosenthal highlighted (Rosenthal, 1966; Rosenthal & Jacobson, 1968) and the
self-fulfilling prophecies that Watzlawick so eloquently describes in his book (Watzlawick, 1984, pp. 95–116) serve to
perpetuate and exacerbate what is happening.

To summarize, it seems to us important that, in any discus-
sions of reality, we take care to differentiate clearly between
two levels, that of the things and events that can reasonably
be taken as being "out there," and that of the varied frameworks through which these are perceived and interpreted.
Also, we believe it to be vital that we never believe what we
believe; that way lies the inquisition. As Feyerabend declares:

> given any rule, however "fundamental" or "necessary" for sci-
> ence, there are always circumstances when it is advisable not
> only to ignore the rule, but to adopt its opposite . . . my thesis
> is that anarchism helps to achieve progress in any one of the
> senses one cares to choose. Even a law-and-order science will
> succeed only if anarchistic moves are occasionally allowed to
> take place. (1978, pp. 23–27)

4

HOW DO WE
UNDERSTAND EMOTIONS?

*To the extent that cognitive factors are potent determinants of
emotional states, it could be anticipated that precisely the same
state of physiological arousal could be labelled "joy" or "fury" or
"jealousy" or any other of a great diversity of emotional labels
depending on the cognitive aspects of the situation.*

— Schachter & Singer (1962, p. 381)

*An emotion is roughly the meaning we give to our felt states of
arousal.*

— Harré & Secord (1972, p. 272)

*It is part of the definition of feeling that it is born in us without
our will, often against our will. As soon as we want to feel . . .
feeling is no longer feeling but an imitation of feeling, a show
of feeling.*

— Kundera (1990, p. 195)

*I think, therefore I am is the statement of an intellectual who
underrates toothaches. I feel, therefore I am is a truth much more
universally valid, and it applies to everything that's alive.*

— Kundera (1990, p. 200)

Another area of human experience that is often considered
to be ignored by brief therapists is that of the emotions. We
agree with Kleckner and her colleagues that the "Unfeeling
Strategic Therapist" is largely a myth. We also agree with
them that it has been the brief/strategic therapists themselves

42

who have been largely responsible for maintaining the secret that they do, in fact, believe that a client's feelings are important. As they point out, "It is not that strategic therapists don't deal with feelings—it's just that they don't talk about it with each other, write about it in the literature, or teach it to trainees" (Kleckner et al., 1992, p. 49).

With our trainees, we have, for some years, been continually pointing out the importance not only of listening to what the client is communicating, including the feelings that are being expressed, but of finding ways of demonstrating to the client that this has been done. Just listening is not necessarily enough. If nothing is fed back, the client cannot know whether he or she has been heard.

A worker in a community health center was seeking help from a consulting therapist. The case was to be observed through a one-way mirror, and the worker was looking forward with some considerable trepidation to the experience.

"I always dread this case coming in. I have no idea where I am going with it."

She described a woman who had been struggling for some time with two out-of-control teenagers and a husband who offered little support, worked long hours, and was prone to violent outbursts. The problem for the worker was that she was finding herself unable to stem what she experienced as an overwhelming tide of bitter complaints that poured endlessly from the woman.

"She never listens to anything I say; will take no advice. She has been thrown out by several agencies, already. I am now the only person left who is still prepared to see her. However, I am really getting nowhere. I know she needs help, but I feel powerless to do anything for her, as well as guilty that I am finding I am beginning actively to dislike her."

While the worker believed she had listened to and understood this woman's predicament, it soon became clear that the client, based on her previous experiences and in the absence of clear feedback from the current situation, believed that nobody was listening to or understanding her problems. Thus she felt constrained hopelessly and helplessly to continue telling her story to anybody who might listen. At the same time, she clearly did not expect that anybody would hear what she was trying to express.

The worker was advised, during the next session, to put aside her notebook, to sit forward in her seat (according to her colleagues, the worker usually sat leaning back when seeing this woman, as though battling against a high wind) and say nothing throughout the whole session, to offer no advice, other than to repeat continually phrases such as:

"This is terrible!"
"How on Earth have you coped over all these years?"
"You must feel that nobody knows what you have been going
     through. You must feel very alone with all this worry."
"How do you keep going in face of all this?"
"Many people would have given up a long time ago."

The woman, gradually began to talk less hurriedly and heatedly, to appear calmer, and to begin to listen to what the worker was saying. Finally, asked once again how it was that she had kept going, the woman smiled and said, "I don't know. Perhaps I'm stronger than I think I am."

By the end of the session, the client was calmer, in a more optimistic frame of mind and prepared to listen to what might be said to her. After the session, the worker declared that she had discovered that she now actually liked and respected the woman. We are aware that the suggestion to the worker could be seen as merely a tactical maneuver offered by the consultant to the worker to help break an impasse, rather than a real example of attending to feelings. This is possibly because, in telling the story of the consultation, the consultant may have neglected to mention the increasing feelings of sadness that affected him as he sat listening to the worker describing the client's story.

It is our belief that clients usually only hear when they feel that they have been heard, when their experiences have been validated, *including* their affective experiences. We believe that a therapist, of whatever school of therapy, must pay sufficient attention to this aspect of a client's experiences for any therapy to be effective. It is in the way that this is done and perhaps in the definition of what amounts to "sufficient attention" that the various therapeutic approaches differ. The expression of feelings is clearly a natural human response and often an important one, particularly at crucial moments of grief, joy, excitement, fear, etc. Where therapies often differ is not only in the extent to which it is seen as important to acknowledge emotions, but also in the extent to which the expression of emotions is believed to play a crucial and central role in the process of therapy and change. It is our belief that, helpful and cathartic though explorations and expressions of emotion can sometimes be, the main mechanism of change is through the ultimate modification of the constructs through which distinctions are made and experience distilled.

It is correct that brief therapists tend to pay considerable attention to the observable. Yet, as George Greenberg highlights in his paper on the contribution of Don Jackson to the field of family therapy,

> While Jackson and his associates, in creating a behavioral format, moved away from mentalistic constructs, they did not deny the existence of internal or intra-psychic mechanisms that influence, alter, and/or facilitate human functioning. In fact, they developed techniques such as "reframing" that were in part designed to affect cognition or "perception." Where they made a major shift was in arguing that one cannot know the perception of another, and that scientifically the best that could be accomplished was to characterize performance, depict behavior, and to operate upon the observable phenomena. (1977, p. 403)

Or, as Arthur Bodin explains,

> *While feelings and thoughts are viewed as important, behavior is viewed as the bottom line in the family therapy of MRI. It is only through behavior that affective and cognitive experiences and events are manifested.* (1981, p. 292)

To a greater or lesser extent, in every sphere of our lives, our feelings are an ever-present phenomenon and are powerful determinants in how we react or fail to react to situations. It has been suggested that our feelings are interpretations of states of physiological arousal, the body's way of preparing for action, that are largely dependent on the various levels of constructs we bring to bear in making sense of the current situation and, based on memories of past experiences, are dependent also on what we *expect* to feel. They are also affected by the prescriptions and proscriptions of the social context and by imperatives associated with gender (Crawford et al., 1992). Whatever the feeling we ultimately experience, the physiological concomitants of the state of arousal, in terms of adrenalin surge, blood pressure, heart-rate, muscle tone, etc., are largely identical. The work of Schachter and Singer supported their proposition that,

> Cognitions arising from the immediate situation as interpreted by past experience provide the framework from within which one understands and labels his feelings. It is the cognition which determines whether the state of physiological arousal will be labelled as "anger," "joy," "fear," or whatever. (1962, p. 380)

Where there is more than one frame for interpreting any experience, there are a number of ways, sometimes conflicting, that we might interpret our experience of physiological arousal – that is, there are a number of ways that we might *feel* about it. For example, many of us have had the experience, before going on stage to give a lecture or some other performance, of alternating rapidly between feelings of excitement and eager anticipation, on the one hand, and of high anxiety and a wish that the Earth would swallow us up, on the other. We can both look forward to the completion of a successful appearance as well as, perhaps, fear failure or making a fool of ourselves. Thus, either feeling may be an appropriate interpretation of the high state of physiological arousal that, in most of us, will precede such occasions. Much subsequent research has tested the notion that self-attribution of emotion is related to the way we make sense of what we observe in our own behavior (Bem, 1965, 1968; Nisbett & Schachter, 1966; Storms & Nisbett, 1970).

> I remember supervising a case from behind a one-way mirror and watching a family being "helped to get in touch with" their feelings of anger toward each other. There was no doubt that they were doing this with considerable heat, vigour and apparent authenticity. But were these *really* the feelings of the family members or were they reacting to their only plausible explanation for the high levels of physiological arousal they were experiencing, an explanation that had maybe even been introduced explicitly or implicitly by a therapist operating from the belief that such problems in families arise from out of unexpressed anger? Alarmed at the growing tension in the room, which seemed to be becoming unproductive and potentially dangerous, I intervened and proposed "sadness about how things might have been" as an alternative explanation for their high level of physiological arousal. This frame led, almost instantaneously, to expressions of sadness and a moving process of increasing gentleness and gradual reaffirmation amongst family members. Which were the real feelings? Clearly, either was a sufficient frame for interpreting the family members' experiences of physiological arousal. One frame seemed more helpful as a lens through which to interpret the arousal than the other, at least as far as creating a seemingly constructive, cooperative more optimistic atmosphere during the rest of the session was concerned. (Cade, 1992a, p. 167)

It could be that another explanation might also have "made sense" to the members of this family, such as guilt, betrayal, fear, contempt, etc., and led to a different, yet arguably equally appropriate and authentic expression of feelings.

It is not that we believe that clients are so malleable that any feeling can somehow be foisted onto them. In any situation, particularly in a complex interactional one that has become highly charged, the constructs that are being brought to bear on it by all those involved, in order to explain it, usually represent the tip of the iceberg of the potential incalculable store of memories and associations that *could* be brought to

bear. As Gendlin observes, "Any moment is a myriad richness.
. . . Going through a simple act involves an enormous number
of familiarities, learnings, senses for the situation, understandings of life and people, as well as the many specifics of the
given situation . . . " (1973, p. 370).

It is our belief that, while an acknowledgment of the existence of a variety of strong emotions can be highly therapeutic
in helping people feel validated and understood, it may not be
helpful or therapeutic to encourage the continued expression
of emotions, particularly those that have been "labeled" in
ways that perpetuate a sense of hopelessness or helplessness.
For example, expressions of anger can be potentially helpful
when the anger is about something over which we feel we have
some control, otherwise such expression may simply lead to
an increased sense of impotence and hopelessness. We need
to be wary of reifying emotions in ways that lock people into
negative patterns of thought and action. In the previous example of one of us waiting to go on stage, an interpretation of
either fear or excitement would "fit the bill" to help us explain
our high state of physiological arousal. An acknowledgment
of the fear may help us feel understood, but it is the other
interpretation that leads us towards getting on with the task.

As Kleckner et al. conclude:

> What should be emphasized . . . is that strategic therapists do
> not spend significant amounts of time merely talking about
> feelings or getting clients to recognize and own feelings; they
> concentrate instead on getting clients to express their feelings
> in ways that are more likely to lead to client satisfaction in
> daily life. (1992, p. 49)

5

NEGOTIATING THE PROBLEM

The first step was what counted. Once you've begun a thing, it exercises a terrible authority over you.

—Jules Romain (1973)

All things have small beginnings.

—Marcus Tullius Cicero

The process of assessment is crucial to the direction taken in any therapy and often, ultimately, to its success. Richard Rabkin has used the analogy of chess for thinking about the process of therapy (1977). As with a chess game, the success or failure of therapy is often determined by the opening "moves," the questions asked, the responses elicited, that reflect the "game plan," and the therapist's assumptions.

All explanatory frameworks are metaphors, though they are metaphors that can have very real consequences. We believe that many different frameworks can help guide therapists in their work. However, problems often occur, as we have earlier said, when these frameworks become confused with "reality" and reified. After a time, clients can come to regard their problems and themselves, and their prognosis, in the light of the therapist's beliefs about them, even though these beliefs might have been implicitly rather than explicitly communicated.

A client who had been labeled "borderline personality," was transferring to a new therapist, due to a change of personnel in the agency in which she was receiving therapy. She reported that when she went to see the new therapist, she would often leave very discouraged and depressed. When asked about the difference between therapist styles, she said, "The other therapist is so pessimistic. When I walk in, I may be feeling very good. She tells me that I look depressed, though. Then I start wondering if, indeed, I am depressed. By the end of the session with her, I definitely am depressed, whether I was to start with or not."

Traditionally, the process of assessment or diagnosis is one in which the client's or the family's problem is "objectively" studied, identified, and described, following which it is treated. Since we view reality as socially mediated, it should be no surprise that we view problems and their definitions (and the pragmatic effects of those definitions) as, to a large extent, socially and interactionally mediated, a process in which the client(s) and therapist together create a "reality" (regardless of the extent to which the participants are aware of this). The degree of influence the client will have in the creation of this "reality," or be seen by the therapist as competent to have, will vary from approach to approach.

Behavior therapists "discover" behavioral problems; analysts "discover" intrapsychic problems, their origins often in childhood; biologically oriented psychiatrists "discover" evidence of neurological problems and chemical deficits; structural/strategic therapists "discover" hierarchical ambiguities and coalitions; contextual therapists "discover" the effects of intergenerational injustice and exploitation; brief therapists "discover" self-reinforcing patterns of thought and action. Each can operate from the assumption that he or she has discovered the fundamental cause of the problem (and, sadly, can often disregard or even scorn other models and explanations, a tendency from which our field has not, by any means, been entirely free).

Everything we think, feel, and do can be seen as embedded in and affected by a complex hierarchy of influences. These range from the wider socio/political level to the individual genetically or environmentally derived neurosynaptic level; from the historical background out of which we come, through our varied experiences of the present (family, peer group, community, gender, racial, etc.), to our future, as we currently anticipate it. For example, considering the complexity of the phenomenon we call schizophrenia, Scheflen shows how it must be viewed as reflecting a complex of influences from a minimum of at least eight different levels (1981). These levels coincide closely with the eight levels of explanation proposed by the biologist Steven Rose as minimally necessary for understanding the behavior of the brain (1976, p. 30).

Scheflen	*Rose*
The societal perspective	Sociological
The institutional level	Social psychological
The family level	Psychological (mentalistic)
Dyadic interaction	Physiological (systems)
Body states and emotionality	Physiological (units)
Physiological subsystems	Anatomical-biochemical
The organization of the nervous system	Chemical
The neural microstructure	Physical

The richness and complexity of this existential tapestry means that any aspect of our being, including the development and maintenance of problems, can be seen as reflecting phenomena existing at any or all of these levels. The richness and complexity of this existential tapestry also means that "evidence" can be found to support a wide range of diagnostic preconceptions. It also means, in our view, that the identification of the "real" cause or causes of any problem can never conclusively be determined.

Brief therapists focus primarily on the observable, on what can be described in a clear and concrete way in terms of things and events. O'Hanlon and Wilk have referred to "descriptive statements based on observation, which neither contain or presuppose any information that could not in principle be derived without interpretation from a video with a sound track" (1987, p. 20). It is not that we deny the complexity of human experience. We believe that the further we move away from the observable or describable nuts and bolts of human interaction, the more we risk becoming caught up in our own metaphors and thus imposing them onto our clients. Also, unless we are operating as agents of social control, it is the specific problem the client brings to us, and in respect of which he or she is a customer, or a potential customer, for therapy, that gives us a mandate to do our job. It may be, at times, that the initial problem brought is being used as a "calling card," and the client is actually more concerned with another problem in respect of which he or she needs time and a greater sense of the trustworthiness and the competence of the therapist before being prepared to broach it. However, though we believe it is our responsibility to provide such a climate, it is ultimately the client who must define the focus. People will not work toward changes for which they are not a customer, however necessary, desirable, or beneficial those changes may seem to be to us or to the others in their lives.

We see traditional notions of resistance as unnecessary in this approach. Although we all tend to stick to "the devil we know" when facing the prospect of significant change, it is our view that people in trouble *want* to change though they may not know how to or, knowing how, may not be able, for a range of individual or interpersonal reasons, to start the process off without some help.

The Brief Therapy Center group in Palo Alto (Fisch et al., 1982; Watzlawick et al., 1974; Weakland et al., 1974) have discussed this crucial subject of customership. Who wants help, with what, or for whom? Sometimes the person who comes to therapy is a customer for changes in another person, a spouse or a child, and is unable or unprepared to see that they themselves could or should make changes in their approach to that person. Often, the person who comes to therapy has been sent by someone else (a school counselor, a probation officer, a court, a parent, a spouse, etc.) and can be quite unmotivated for, even hostile to, the idea of therapy. This does not necessarily mean that nothing can be done, but that the therapist must begin cautiously from a respectful, one-down position, without making any assumptions. Much of what is often defined as "resistance" can be viewed as the direct result of a therapist failing to clarify whether somebody is a customer or not and thus trying to "sell" something to a person who is currently not interested in buying anything. Alternatively, the person might possibly be interested in buying something but not what the therapist is currently attempting to sell or not while other people (including, in their view, the therapist) are attempting to persuade or to coerce them, for reasons of their own, into "making such a purchase."

A man made an appointment on the recommendation of his insurance agent, who had apparently told him that he could be hypnotized to make him stop smoking. He was informed that he had been lied to; the therapist could not and would not make him stop smoking. However, he might be able to help him stop, but first wanted to know if the man himself wanted to stop smoking. He replied that he did not. Asked if he had ever experienced breathing or health difficulties related to his smoking, he said that he hadn't really suffered any untoward effects. On leaving the Navy forty years earlier, the doctors had told him that he wouldn't last three years because of his extreme drinking and smoking habits. He was now a retired man and had given up drinking alcohol and cut out the fat in his diet on doctor's orders several years before. Smoking was one of the few pleasures he had left to him. He was due to see his doctor for a physical in a few weeks.

The therapist told him that, from what he had said, if the doctor recommended that he quit smoking, he would probably be able to quit with little trouble, just as he had done with alcohol. If the doctor did not make such a recommendation, he should continue to enjoy smoking for as long as he wanted. He said, "Thank you, young man. I guess I didn't really want to quit, and our talk has helped me realize that. It was the insurance man who wanted me to stop."

The therapist wished him well and told him that his door was always open if he wished to return.

The following outlines the important aspects of customership as presented initially by the Palo Alto group and as subsequently adapted by Steve de Shazer and his colleagues (de Shazer, 1988):

A *visitor* (defined also by Fisch et al., 1982, as a "window shopper") is uncommitted, often involved in therapy under some kind of duress, implicit or explicit, and usually because of the concerns of others. However clear it may be to those others or to us that this person has problems, he or she has no agenda to talk, in the current context, about problems or to receive help. Any attempt at intervention is, therefore, likely to be fruitless or to lead to what could subsequently be called "resistance." Steve de Shazer's advice in such situations is respectful listening, compliments where possible, but no suggestions or tasks.

A *complainant* has a particular problem (or list of problems), specific or vague, either concerning themselves or about some other person(s) and about which they are usually prepared to talk, sometimes at length. However, although they may either see themselves as being relatively powerless, or as having the potential to influence the problem(s) through their own actions, it is not yet clear that the therapist is being invited directly to offer advice or help to them (or they may take the position that it is up to the other person(s) to change, not them, in which case they should probably be treated initially as a visitor, with empathy, but offered no tasks or suggestions).

A *customer* is someone who comes in with a complaint, about themselves or about some other person(s), of which it is possible to gain a relatively clear description, and about which he or she quite clearly wishes to do something and for which the therapist's help is being sought.

It is important not to see these definitions as describing fixed and real "characteristics" of clients, but purely guidelines for thinking about *the therapy relationship*. They describe positions adopted by clients *in relation to* the positions, or the anticipated positions, taken by therapists, and by other family members or professionals involved. This stands in contrast with traditional notions of "resistance," which is seen to be a quality that resides "within" clients.

It is common for members of a family to adopt different positions vis-à-vis each other, and also to vary in the positions they adopt both vis-à-vis each other or the therapist within a session or from one session to another. For example, a woman might bring her reluctant husband in for therapy. She is clearly a customer for him to change. He has no interest in therapy and is clearly only there to keep the peace, or to be in a position to say, "Well, I went along; but it did no good, just like I said it wouldn't."

On finding the therapist does not tell him the error of his ways and shows understanding, the husband may well become a customer for therapy by the end of the session. However, because what has happened was not what she was expecting, the wife may have moved into the complainant position or even have become a visitor (at least, for this therapist at this time). Sometimes, people will remain visitors until other people in their lives, family, friends, or other professionals, stop pressuring them to come to therapy. They can then come with their own agenda and the therapist can more easily avoid the difficult position of appearing to be the agent of those others.

Of course, it is possible to have several customers at once, each with different problems. This situation often occurs in family and marital therapy, where more than one person is seen in the session and each may have his or her own different, sometimes conflicting, agenda and problems.

For example, a family might seek therapy with the impetus initially coming from the parents, who are complaining about the behavior and attitude of their 15-year-old daughter. She has repeatedly broken several family and household rules, skipping school, staying out all night, and entering into frequent arguments with the parents. The daughter is likely initially to be reluctant to attend therapy, until the therapist might ask her (with or without the parents present) if she would like help getting her parents off her back. It is probable that she would indeed be interested in this and it then becomes possible to dovetail and align the two sets of goals. The parents want the daughter to obey the family rules, and the daughter wants fewer conflicts with her parents and less restrictions. Here we have two problems and sets of goals with two distinct "customers."

After ensuring that one has a customer in therapy, the next question to be addressed is: What is the customer's problem?

That is, what behavior or experience is occurring in the person's life that they would like to lessen or eliminate or, alternatively, what behavior or experience is *not* occurring that they would like to have feature more regularly in their life? In some approaches, the decision as to what problem the client has is based on a theory of pathology rather than on that for which the client asks for help. We are interested in clear problem definition in terms of actual behaviors. Rather than accepting the use of predicates such as "He is naughty" or "I am depressed," questions such as "What exactly does he do that you consider naughty?" or "How does your feeling of sadness affect your behavior?" can encourage a more detailed analysis. It is also often important to find out when the problem started, how often, when and where it occurs, in relation to whom or what, etc. Then the attempted solutions need to be as clearly elicited.

Because brief therapy assessment is oriented toward the present and the future (what does the client/customer not like in the present and what do they want to change in the future), we do not usually search for causes or antecedents to the problem in the past, although we recognize that, for some people, a framework for understanding the effects of past events can help the process of revising personal constructs. Rather, when looking for a description of the problem, we concentrate on the present or the recent past. We are searching for the internal, individual, and interactional patterns associated with the problem. We also want to understand exactly what the client is describing, so we do not have to make guesses, which may be inaccurate.

Brief therapists tend to be interested either in what is not working for people in order to find ways of persuading them to try something different, or finding out what is already working so that people can be encouraged to do more of it. They also tend to be more focused on the future and upon solutions than on etiology and the past or even, sometimes, the present (de Shazer, 1988, 1991; Furman & Ahola, 1992; O'Hanlon & Weiner-Davis, 1989).

The following is a list of the areas we would tend to ask questions about when seeking clear problem definition, together with what appear to be the important sequences surrounding the problem. We will look in more detail at the future-focused approaches later on.

When Does the Problem Occur?

We search for any regularities involving the timing of the problem. Are there any times when the problem usually or always happens or, alternatively, when it never happens? Is there a specific time of the day, week, month, or year when the problem more frequently or less frequently occurs?

Where Does the Problem Occur?

Is there any place where the problem always occurs or is more likely to occur? Is there any place where the problem never occurs? We will often ask about general locations: for example, at work, at school, or at home, and about specific locations, such as the particular room of the house in which the problem is most likely to occur.

What Is the Performance of the Problem?

If we could watch a videotape of the problem in action, what would we see when it was happening? What specific postures and gestures, sequences of actions, interactions, talk, etc., would we see and hear if we were watching a performance of the problem?

With Whom Does It Occur?

Who is more likely to be around when the problem occurs? What do those other people do and say before, during, and after the problem behavior occurs? What do these others say about the person who has the problem or about the problem itself?

What Are the Exceptions
to the Rule of the Problem?

Rarely does a problem occur all the time, so we often pursue a line of inquiry that highlights reports of things that interfere with the problem, interrupt it, or happen instead of it. de Shazer has articulated this method in his solution-focused work (de Shazer, 1988, 1991). His method involves inviting the person both to notice and then do more of the exceptions to the problem so the exception becomes the rule that is substituted for the rule of the problem. In a similar way, White looks for what he calls unique outcomes (1988).

What Does the Client (or Clients) Do
Differently, or What Activities Are
Prevented, Because of the Problem?

How does the problem interfere with people doing what they would usually be doing or would like to do? Sometimes, in order to get this information, we ask people what they would be doing differently if the problem were resolved. de Shazer has described the use of the "Miracle Question" as a way not only of eliciting answers to this question but also of giving people the experience of talking in terms of solution as though it was inevitable or it had already started (de Shazer, 1988, 1991).

What Does the Client
Show in the Session That
Is Related to the Problem?

Sometimes clients show evidence of some part of the problem in the therapist's office. This is almost always true in marital and family sessions, where the process of the problem unfolds before the therapist's eyes and ears, but it can also be true in individual sessions.

A client complained about not being accepted by colleagues in his professional career. During the first session, he spoke so loudly that, after the session, therapists from nearby offices complained that they could hear what he said through the entire session. He also looked all around the room except at the therapist, so much so that it became quite noticeable. At the beginning of the next session, the therapist reported what the other therapists had said and wondered whether the loud voice and the avoidance of eye contact might have something to do with the trouble with his colleagues. He responded by telling the therapist that his boss had once mentioned that he spoke too loudly, but nobody else ever had, and so he had just dismissed it as his boss being highly critical. We decided that he would try speaking more softly in the next week and for him to notice how his colleagues responded. He discovered that it worked well. For the next week, he concentrated on making eye contact and that also worked well.

What Are the Client's Explanations and Frames Regarding the Problem?

People often have ideas about what caused or causes their difficulties or what the problem means in their lives. As we have earlier commented, these explanations and frames of reference may be helpful or may be part of the problem. In either case, it is a good idea to assess what they are.

What do clients believe caused or causes the problem? What, if any, do they think are the deeper difficulties this problem reflects? What does this problem indicate about their identities or their anticipated futures? What metaphors, analogies, or images do clients use when talking about the problem? Also, what are, or have been, the explanations of significant others, such as family members or other involved professionals, which may have guided their attitudes toward and treatment of clients and also affected clients' ways of thinking about the problem? Nowadays, it can sometimes be important to find out what self-help books clients have read.

What Are the Client's or Others' Attempted Solutions Regarding the "Problem"?

We have looked earlier at how problems can be seen as reflecting the way that clients have persisted in using inappropriate and unsuccessful solutions. What have clients and the significant others in their lives (including therapists) been doing to attempt to solve the problem?

How Will We Know When We Get There?

Of crucial importance for the brief therapist is helping clients to clarify and express goals. In the words of a book title, *If You Don't Know Where You're Going, You'll Probably End Up Somewhere Else.*

We have clients teach us about their images and ideas about how they'll know when the problem has been resolved. What will be happening in other areas of their lives when the problem no longer plagues them? Sometimes, just being asked about the future and envisioning a better future can help clients to see their way clear to solving their problems. Sometimes, it just helps us be clearer on what it is they want. Sometimes, as de Shazer and his colleagues have suggested (de Shazer et al., 1986), the therapy can concentrate primarily on what the solutions will look like and work toward the realization of those solutions without ever reaching a clear description of what the problem is. Either way, this is an important part of the assessment process for us. Since we have no general explanatory models or normative models to guide us, clients' goals and visions of the future become our compass settings and help us map our way to their hoped-for destinations. We try to focus on a clearly described goal as early as we can without alienating the client. If we receive messages, either verbal or nonverbal, that the client is irritated with our focus on goals, we either explain our purpose or back off and refocus on what they are indicating they consider is more important to discuss.

> Example: "This may seem a funny place to start, but I always like to know where I'm going, so I can listen better for what will be helpful to you. So, if you can, tell me what you hope will be happening in your life when we've been successful in here. What will you be doing after therapy? How will others know you've changed? How will you know?

In order to be achievable, it is preferable that clients be encouraged to formulate goals in terms that can be checked. Well-formed goals consist of clients' actions, or conditions that can be brought about by clients' actions. Often they include time elements: how often (frequency); when (date/time/deadline); where and for how long (duration).

To be workable, we think the goal must be mutual. Client and therapist must agree that the goal is relevant and achievable. If there is more than one client, or the customer is not the client, it is preferable if all parties can agree that the goal is relevant and achievable.

To ensure that all parties know when the goal is achieved, we help clients translate vague, nonsensory-based words and phrases into action-based language. One must be able to imagine the goal as if it could be viewed/heard on a videotape player. Of course, clients often initially talk about goals in vague ways or in ways that refer more to feelings or inner states. As we have highlighted earlier, we consider it important to listen to descriptions of feelings and inner states or qualities, and to demonstrate empathy. However, we will continue respectfully to encourage descriptions of outer (observable) correlates for these states.

If a person complained about being shy, we would ask them to describe a typical interaction (or lack of interaction) with others. Does the person look at the ground when others are around? Does he or she sit alone at a party? Does he or she refuse invitations to parties? We would use these action descriptions and work to encourage the person to change the actions and interactions we and they consider the most relevant and most likely to result in overall change.

> An anorexic young woman was finding it difficult to be more specific in defining goals other than "I will be feeling better." Finally, through the use of the Miracle Question, she was able to identify as initial goals being able to look into a full-length mirror on her way to the shower, and choosing something to wear based on what she liked rather than what was most concealing. She was advised to attempt these only when ready. At the next session, she wore a sleeveless dress and described herself as feeling more optimistic about the future.

To assist and lead our clients, we often provide multiple choice answers when they hesitate in stating clear goals or when they continue to answer our queries about their goals with vague words and phrases. For example,

> "Do you think, maybe, that the first signs of things improving might be that you'll actually look at yourself in the mirror rather than avert your eyes, or that you might decide to wear something because it looks good rather than because it best conceals you? Or will it be something else?"

Sometimes it is important for us to inform clients that we are searching for an achievable goal and to give them a rationale for our search.

> "I keep going back to this issue of how we'll know when we've been successful and can stop meeting because I want to be sure of what it is we are working toward."

> "I become concerned that what we're doing in here could become (or has become) part of the problem instead of the solution. I think defining a goal will help avoid that because we'll have a clearly defined stopping place."

When we ask about goals, we take the opportunity to create an expectancy of change and results. Our words reflect that expectancy. We use words like "will," "when," "yet," when speaking about the client's therapy (or post-therapy) goals.

"So you haven't asked a woman out for a date yet, and you'd like to be able to get into a relationship?"

"So, when you're feeling better, less depressed or not depressed, you'll be getting up earlier and spending more time with friends?"

Constructing a Solvable Problem

An important goal when negotiating the problem is for difficulties to be defined, through the evolving discourse between therapist and client(s), in a way that maximizes them being able to be acted upon. As we have already said, this is more likely to happen when specific behaviors rather than predicates or hypothetical entities are invoked. A child who refuses to tidy her room is easier to deal with than a "naughty child"; a person who pours his first drink on first returning home from work is easier to deal with than an "alcoholic"; a couple who have not yet found a way of insisting that a fearful child go to school is easier to deal with than "an enmeshed family"; a lack of experience at relating to peers is easier to deal with than "low self-esteem"; a tendency to avoid contact with others and to cry frequently is easier to deal with than "depression."

To take but one of these examples, a person who pours out a first drink on returning home from work each evening might be persuaded instead to take the dog for a walk as the first thing he does each evening.

The reader is invited to practice breaking down any frequently used diagnostic category into a pattern of discrete personal and interpersonal behaviors that repeats under a particular set of circumstances such that elements in the pattern might more easily be acted upon. This process is far more important, however, than just a matter of pragmatics. The implications of invoking ultimately unprovable entities such as, for example, "co-dependency" or "addictive personalities," "psychological damage" or "attention deficit disorder," to name but four categories from a very long list, can be profound and, to us, somewhat frightening (although potentially good for profits).

6

NEUTRALITY AND POWER, SUGGESTIONS, TASKS, AND PERSUASION

People are generally better persuaded by the reasons which they have themselves discovered than by those which have come into the minds of others.

—Pascal

It is our very simple minded belief that if you do not choose to influence, if the word strategy gets stuck in your throat as you attempt to utter it, or if you believe that human beings are capable of not influencing one another (either intentionally or unintentionally), you should retreat from human society.

—Brooks & Heath (1989, p. 320)

Brief therapists typically make frequent use of direct suggestions and tasks and, therefore, must become adept at the art of persuasion. It is arguable that the art of therapy, whatever the approach used, has much in common with the art of persuasion. For many, this will be an unpalatable fact. Yet, whether we like it or not, we are a profession concerned primarily with encouraging people, directly or indirectly, to change either their attitudes or their behaviors.

INFLUENCE AND EXPERTISE

There is a belief, currently held by many in our field, that it is possible to avoid influence and merely to listen to a client's or a family's story, to encourage a discourse in which the therapist makes no attempt to "direct, maneuver or change the family's dialogue in a particular direction . . . " (Markowitz, 1992, p. 12, quoting Harlene Anderson). We believe this to be a dangerous delusion. It is arguably impossible to avoid betraying opinions and influencing the interaction, albeit unconsciously, through the whole range of vocal and nonvocal channels of communication through which information can be exchanged. For example, whatever our therapeutic model may be, we choose to respond to one statement and not to another, we ask a particular question and not a different one, we nod or say "mmm" in response to a particular statement and not to another. In each of these cases, we are influencing the process and direction of the interaction. Much will be communicated through subtle levels of facial expression, eye movements, pupil dilation, breathing patterns, posture, etc., that we are totally unaware of and thus unable to control. It is our concern that such subtle levels of influence are likely to be all the more insidious in that they operate outside of the awareness of all concerned. We clearly agree with anything that increases a client's sense of autonomy, of self-determination, of their own abilities. We do not agree, however, that for the therapist to make suggestions or to persuade the client to try something different represents manipulation or the imposition and exploitation of an unhealthy power differential.

There appears also to be a current preoccupation in our field (dare we say, sometimes a somewhat sanctimonious one) with denying completely the validity of the role of "expert," or even of expertise itself. Maturana's tautologous assertion about the impossibility of *instructive interaction* is often invoked; and *"the conversation"* has been elevated to the level of the sacramental, to be referred to reverently in hushed tones. The taking of such an expert role is seen variously as epistemologically unsound (whatever that means), as presumptuous, as elitist, as encouraging dependency, as holding onto and exercising professional power, as controlling the "power of knowledge," etc., etc. While we are sure that there are some therapists for whom this might be the case, we would argue that the role of "expert" can also be taken in such a way that it does not dis-empower (in fact, it is not possible to empower, only to avoid that which dis-empowers).

It has not escaped our notice that most of those who are eschewing expertise and technique are extremely experienced therapists with much expertise and a finely honed command of technique. We agree with the move away from adversarial attitudes, covertly manipulative techniques, and the attitude that therapy is a process in which we, with all the know-how, act benevolently upon those without. However, we believe that to pretend to have no knowledge or skills, or to deny that the experience and wisdom we bring to our therapy was gained through the prolonged and sometimes painful exercise of and evolution in that knowledge and those skills, is nonsense. To offer the fruits of many years of experience in a sensitive and respectful way to a troubled client or family is not necessarily synonymous with disempowering them or treating them as incompetent (although it clearly can be done in that way).

As just one example, Brian often announces to individuals, couples, and families that, over the last 25 years or so, he has become a considerable expert in those approaches that *usually do not work* in relationships, particularly where they have become a regular feature of those relationships. He usually goes on to declare that, in respect of what *does* work, he is far less able to make such a definitive statement. However, he admits that he will often have a few ideas about what *might* work, many of them borrowed from previous clients, some of them ideas of his own, and which he would be quite happy to share with them (Cade, 1992b).

NEUTRALITY

The issue of neutrality has received considerable attention and has caused some controversy over the last few years. The therapist's position of neutrality is, in our view, necessitated by the *pragmatic* requirements for being therapeutic when working at the interface of relationships. A loss of neutrality usually pulls a therapist into an unhelpful position. Taking a neutral position for therapeutic considerations is not necessarily an expression of the therapist's personal opinion of, or attitude toward or about, any particular person, behavior, set of values, attitude, or event. Our development of the use of the position arose by learning from the cases in which we failed to be helpful by allowing ourselves to take sides, sometimes believing it was important to protect one of the parties, sometimes unwittingly, sometimes fooling ourselves that we were being therapeutically provocative in order to "unbalance" the system, sometimes by "grinding our own axes."

There are those in our field who seem to equate neutrality in therapy with the adoption of a detached, noncommittal, unemotional stance. We have seen some therapists interviewing families while employing a Buster Keaton approach to emotional expressiveness. It seems to us possible to retain a neutral position in respect of two sides by adopting approaches from anywhere on a continuum ranging from a remote, noncommittal stance in respect of both, to taking a warm, concerned, affirming, engaged, even friendly, position in respect of both. The important thing is that, over time, neither side be treated differently such that an alliance be implicitly or explicitly formed with one against the other. Therapeutic neutrality can mean being on neither side *or* both sides.

Neutrality in respect of outcome is again, in our view, a *pragmatic* position that it is important to take in some situations, not necessarily an expression of the therapist's lack of interest in a resolution of problems, or an insensitivity to wider sociopolitical issues. Often, when a therapist becomes too clearly identified with the arguments in favor of a change, whether that position be explicitly or implicitly communicated, he or she can become, as it were, the main "customer" for how a family or how a particular family member should be. It is as though the therapist has then colonized those arguments, leaving available to the family member(s) only the counter-arguments to that change, together with the accompanying affect produced by those counter-arguments. The rights and wrongs of the therapist's view of how things *ought to be* become irrelevant if the pursuit of those ends, however benignly motivated, has the effect of disempowering people, increasing their "resistance," or further entrenching their attitudes. Considering the therapy of families in which abuse has occurred, Kearney, Byrne, and McCarthy have referred to the "colonizing potential" of the professional networks involved with troubled or troublesome families from impoverished and marginalized communities. They point out that "such families are singularly exposed to recursive crusades of invasion and retreat under benevolent banners of control and treatment ... the colonized, sustained by the sanctions of the colonizer, maintain their ambivalent partnership in oscillations of revolt and acquiescence" (Kearney et al., 1989, p. 17). We will look further at this process of colonization when looking at paradoxical techniques.

We prefer to use the framework of visitor, complainant, and customer, referred to in an earlier chapter, for considering these issues, rather than the more generic notion of neutrality. In our opinion, by keeping continually in mind the question "Who is actually the customer for what?" we can usually avoid making unhelpful alliances, becoming too enthusiastic or dogmatic about how others should be, and, perhaps more seriously, "grinding our own axes." In circumstances in which people are clearly motivated to change aspects of their lives, we are more than happy to act as cheerleaders in respect of their attempts to be different (though we usually draw the line at wearing short skirts and waving pom-poms).

In private practice, we rarely face directly the issue of having to adopt a social control stance. However, we are clear that, if we had to take such a stance, we would not be acting as a therapist in respect of the person(s) toward whom we were taking it (even though the action may, itself, be therapeutic, even vital, in the short term, say to a child or a woman at risk, or to a person who might be saved from doing something they might subsequently regret). We think we must always be careful to keep the two hats separate. When a social control position is adopted, it is clearly either the therapist, or some party or power that the therapist represents, who is the customer for something to happen. In our experience, people do not change except in ways they *themselves* are customers for. Where we are constrained to take the customer role, particularly where we have sanctions that we can bring into operation, we are essentially seeking obedience (in certain circumstances, this may be the only and the correct option; but we should never confuse it with therapy). However, this does not mean that it is not possible to seek to perform the social control function in as "therapeutic" a manner as possible (Weakland & Jordan, 1990).

SUGGESTIONS, TASKS, AND PERSUASION

In brief therapy, we often ask people to experiment with new behaviors or to entertain new ways of thinking about their situations which sometimes represent radical departures from how they are used to behaving or from what they have long cherished as self-evident truths or as "common sense." The strength of a person's attitudes, beliefs, and values will be important variables in the extent to which they will be prepared to try something new. Rokeach has elaborated a three-level hierarchy of beliefs ranging from the most primitive, deeply held, and basic (level 1) through those beliefs connected with the various authorities governing to whom we will listen and to whom we will afford respect (level 2), to those beliefs that are relatively peripheral (level 3). The more a behavior or attitude is anchored in beliefs from level 1, the more strength and intensity with which it is held, the more difficult it is likely to be to influence it (Rokeach, 1968). In the rest of this chapter we are going to present some ideas from research into the art of persuasion, which we consider relevant to our work as therapists.

Clearly, people are usually more likely to cooperate and to try something new when validated and when they feel that their beliefs and feelings are understood and respected. Alternatively, people who feel misunderstood, particularly when they are experiencing high levels of distress or anxiety, tend to be far less able to concentrate on persuasive messages regardless of how relevant the messages appear to be (to the sender) or how the messages are being transmitted (Nunnally & Bobren, 1959).

A highly distressed woman who had just been deserted by her husband was being advised by a group of concerned workers that she should contact her lawyer and also the social security department. She sat sobbing in the agency's reception area, seemingly incapable of action. It was not until one of the workers acknowledged and validated the woman's feelings of fear, anger, and despair and invited her to take however long she needed, that she almost immediately asked for the telephone number of the social security department and a directory so that she could look up the number of her lawyer. So, at the risk of repeating ourselves, it is important that we not only listen to what we are being told by our clients, either explicitly or implicitly, but that we also say things that indicate that we have listened and that demonstrate our understanding of the stories they are telling us and that acknowledge their feelings about those stories.

People are more likely to comply with requests or suggestions that are consistent with their wishes, experiences, and attitudes. "In persuasion, the greater the congruence between the belief or action advocated and the felt need of the persuadee, the higher the probability that persuasion will occur" (Brooks & Heath, 1989, p. 333). A young woman referred herself because she was making herself ill from excessive worrying and studying for her final exams. She had recently had to be carried out from a trial examination, after being violently sick from anxiety and exhaustion. She knew that she had already done more than enough preparation to pass "with flying colors," but she could not relax. It was suggested that, each day, she toss a coin. Whenever it came up heads, she was forbidden to do any work at all on that day. However hard it might be for her to do so, she was to go to the beach or somewhere similar, and under no circumstance was she to take any text books with her. Whenever the coin came up tails, she could study as hard as she felt was appropriate.

She was able successfully to slow down. She survived the exams and achieved the highest marks in her year. This suggestion worked, we feel, because it was totally congruent with the wishes of the young woman to slow down. Had she wanted help to deal with her panic such that she could work even harder, the suggestion would clearly not have worked, however much we believed that it would have been the best thing for her to do.

People who hold rigid, dogmatic ideas tend to reject ideas that are not in agreement with the sources of authority from which they draw their beliefs and attitudes.

> if one has to convince a very dogmatic person . . . one must keep in mind that the receiver will not necessarily be persuaded by logic or evidence, or by new ideas. Rather, this type of person can be influenced by appealing to his or her authority figures and to traditional values, and by keeping in mind that he or she has a rigid belief system that does not tolerate much inconsistency. (Bettinghaus & Cody, 1987, p. 48)

An ex-soldier announced that he was an extremely traditional person who did not even believe women had yet earned the right to vote. He believed that a family should run on discipline and that it was his wife's attitudes that were undermining his authority such that the children were running wild. It was clear he had come to see the therapist in order to prove to his wife that therapists could be of no help. The man was asked whether he saw himself as being like a First World War general or a Second World War general. He asked for clarification. It was explained that the former had learned little over four years and seemed to have had little interest in the morale of their troops or in saving lives. At the end of the war they were still doing the same things that had clearly shown themselves to be totally ineffective right from the beginning of the war. The latter, however, learned from their experiences, payed considerable attention to matters of morale and to the limiting of casualties, and were adaptive to changing circumstances. After considering the question for a few moments, the man thoughtfully admitted, "I guess I've become a bit like a First World War general."

Clearly, to have confronted this man with the error of his thinking would have been unlikely to have been helpful. However, once a distinction between different styles of generalship had been drawn, he could be encouraged to explore, from within his own constructs, the implications of becoming more like a Second World War general. As Miller points out, "From a pragmatic vantage point, messages seeking to shape and condition responses may have a higher likelihood of success than communications aiming at converting established behavioral patterns" (1980, p. 19).

A couple came to a therapist to ask him to help them prevent their twenty-six-year-old son from making a relationship with a divorced woman. The husband professed strong Christian beliefs and was morally outraged by his son's behavior. The therapist agreed with them about the heavy load that God has asked parents to bear, and discussed with them the parable of the prodigal son. He pointed out how much faith had been needed by the father in the parable to allow his son to waste his inheritance and learn by his mistakes and yet still welcome him back and forgive him. No attempt was made to link up the meaning of the parable with any suggestion that the man change his attitude. At the following session the man showed he had been deeply moved by the previous session, had re-read the parable, and had taken his wife to meet the woman concerned and both had found her to be basically "a good woman." (Cade, 1980b, p. 97)

In this example, the man was helped through the use of a parable from the Bible spontaneously to "discover" new attitudes that were both consistent with and had grown out of the teachings of his own strongly-held beliefs. To have tried overtly to persuade him to change his attitudes or to have indicated what conclusions he should draw from the parable, would probably have served only to harden those attitudes.

Self-generated arguments are far more influential than arguments produced by others, and it appears that the more arguments that are self-generated in favor of a position, the more likely it is that that position will persist. It also appears that, when considering a series of persuasive messages, people remember with much more clarity their own thoughts and their own arguments than the messages themselves (whether they were in favor of or against those messages). As Perloff and Brock observe,

> individuals are active participants in the persuasion process who attempt to relate message elements to their existing repertoires of information. In so doing, these individuals may consider materials that are not actually contained in the persuasive message. These self-generated cognitions may agree with the position advocated by the source or they may disagree. Insofar as the communication elicits favorable cognitive responses, attitudes should change in the direction advocated by the source. To the extent that the message evokes unfavorable mental reactions, attitude change in the direction advocated by the source should be inhibited. (1980, p. 69)

The implications of this, as Perloff and Brock go on to say, are that "once communicators have started to change people's minds about an issue, then they can be most assured that this change will persist if audience members rehearse their own thoughts about the message rather than the speaker's arguments" (1980, p. 85).

The major effect of self-confrontation is on subjects whose initial values are *congruent* with those values implicit or explicit in a persuasive message even though they may be behaving in ways that are not (Grube et al., 1977). Where the values of a client are not congruent with those informing the message, confrontation is far less effective. In fact, where the message evokes unpleasant, unfavorable, or disapproving reactions through the extent of the incongruity, attitude and behavior change in the direction advocated will tend to be inhibited and counter-arguments generated (which may or may not be openly expressed).

Also, anticipatory counter-argumentative responses will be produced and rehearsed in advance when a person expects, or is warned of, an upcoming persuasive message that is likely to run counter to his or her values and attitudes, making the person much less susceptible to persuasion (Petty & Cacioppo, 1977).

A man, a retired sailor, had been defined by several previous workers of various disciplines as rigid and Victorian in his ideas about discipline, as totally resistant and without motivation. He viewed his 14-year-old daughter as disobedient, uncouth, and out of control. The previous workers considered the girl to be quite normal, driven to "act out" and to rebel by her father's rigid attitudes and expectations. Her mother's attempts to keep the peace and to defend her daughter led only to increased tension. There was some official concern that the situation could become violent and that the girl was at risk. The father was defined as totally unable to see how his attitudes were at the root of the problem. He had expressed the opinion that social work and psychiatry were "worse than useless."

Referred to a brief therapist, the man demonstrated by his demeanor that he was not prepared to cooperate other than merely to attend. The therapist commented to the father on how difficult it was bringing up children in this more permissive era. Many of the old traditional values seemed to have been lost. He declared his belief that parents had a right to define what was appropriate behavior in their homes, and that youngsters needed the greater experience of their parents, even though they might think of them as "old fashioned." The therapist regretted the loss of many of these old values and principles and the lack of self-respect and self-discipline frequently demonstrated in modern society. "But, of course," he continued, "Good parents will obviously become more flexible and negotiate more as their children grow up."

At this unexpected validation of many of his beliefs, the father began to nod in agreement, including at the final statement about the need to become more flexible. He became increasingly thoughtful and, after a few minutes, leaned forward and said, "I wonder if perhaps I'm too old fashioned; perhaps I'm too hard on her: Perhaps that's the real problem."

The therapist commented cautiously that there seemed to be many parents nowadays who did not seem to care as much about how their children behaved. Children really needed to learn right from wrong. The father nodded again, yet, a few minutes later, began with more insistence to declare his belief that he was probably being unreasonable. "After all, she *is* 14 now; she's not a bad kid really. Times are different now, and I suppose I ought to learn to live with them."

The more the therapist urged caution, the more the father insisted that it was *he* who needed to change. He agreed to another appointment and the outcome of the case was a rapid improvement in the relationship between the man and his daughter.

At the start, the man had doubtless anticipated a "soft and mollycoddling" approach on the part of the therapist to his daughter's behavior and that he would again be told the error of his ways. His counter-arguments had doubtless been well-rehearsed. He had been repeatedly confronted by a succession of workers attempting to persuade him, sometimes gently, sometimes more forcefully, to adopt an approach inconsistent with his apparent beliefs and attitudes.

With his beliefs and concerns validated and experiencing no need to defend his position, he quickly allowed an expansion of that position, accepting the notion that good parents become more flexible as their children grow up. The therapist's expressions of caution and his reluctance to blame the father seemed to encourage the man to generate increasingly more of his own arguments in favor of increased tolerance, arguments that previously he would never have accepted from others. Once his attitudes had begun to modify, he became better able to tolerate and use advice not only from the therapist but also from his wife and his daughter. It was clearly important to him to feel himself to be, and to be seen by others as, a good parent. As Miller points out, "success in shaping the responses of the intended persuadee hinges upon the linkage of those responses to strongly held values . . . " (Miller, 1980, p. 18).

The repetition of a persuasive message might, in the short term, produce agreement and cooperation. However, it will be

inclined rapidly to become counterproductive if the repetition
continues, tending to produce increasing "resistance" the more
it is repeated (Cacioppo & Petty, 1979). Some research has also
suggested that too much positive reinforcement of a person's
attitudes and behavior can actually rebound and inhibit the
influence of a persuasive communication (McGuire, 1964).

For example, a school teacher, following a seminar on behavioral approaches, realized that she had been overreacting to a
young boy's naughtiness and thus may have been unwittingly
reinforcing both the problem behavior and the child's sense of
himself as being bad. She decided to begin giving him more
encouragement and also praising whatever he did that could
be seen as warranting praise and, as far as was possible, under-
reacting to his usual provocative behaviors. She was pleas-
antly surprised at a rapid improvement in his behavior. However, to her surprise and disappointment, the change was
short-lived. She finally sought a consultation about the case
and was advised to continue with her policy of underreaction
to his provocative behaviors but to be much more sparing with
her encouragement and praise. The boy's behavior improved
and, this time, the improvement was maintained.

A person who can be persuaded to agree to a small request
or suggestion is more likely then to agree with larger requests.
This is perhaps not an unfamiliar phenomenon. However, research has also shown that, in many cases, people requested
to perform an action large or even absurd enough to ensure
that it will be rejected, will often immediately accept a smaller
request that seems more reasonable. Without the first request,
the second request would normally have been rejected. Perhaps people are more likely to make concessions to those who
appear to make concessions to them. For example, a severely
agoraphobic woman became petrified when her therapist announced that, this session, she was to walk with him through
the center of a local shopping mall. With considerable relief
she accepted his alternative suggestion that they have a cup
of coffee together at a local café. This was her first trip out of
the house in several months.

Suggested restraint from doing a task or responding to a
suggestion that is nevertheless clearly elaborated can influ-

ence some people toward an attempt to follow the suggestion. For example:

> "Normally, at this stage, I would suggest [here the suggestion is clearly outlined by the therapist] but, at the moment, I am concerned that you should not have a further experience of failure."

It is also possible to use an illusion of alternatives in which two suggestions are made, both of which might be rejected if presented singly, but where one might be attempted if its rejection is made dependent on the acceptance of the other. For example, with the above agoraphobic woman, she could have been posed the question:

> "Would you like to walk around the main shopping center with me and describe your feelings to me, or would you prefer to start off with a shorter trip down to the local café for a cup of coffee?"

For a further elaboration of this approach it is worth studying examples from Milton Erickson's work (Rossi, 1980).

It is also important to consider how to respond to the way people deal with tasks or suggestions. Have they been followed, modified, opposed, ignored, or forgotten? The therapist must be guided by such feedback in order to determine the next step. For example, if suggestions are followed as requested, then further such suggestions are indicated; if opposed, forgotten, or ignored, then the therapist must carefully consider his or her position. Has he or she misjudged the extent to which a client or family is a customer, or has the therapist become more motivated than they are for a particular change? Alternatively, did the client or family come up with a different or a better idea, one that was more appropriate for them? It is our view that the apparent failure of a task or suggestion should normally be seen as the result of a misunderstanding or miscalculation on the part of the therapist rather than as resistance or noncompliance on the part of the client or family.

7

LESS OF THE SAME

. . . if we change some aspect of a system . . . the first result will often be a lot of other changes where we didn't expect them. . . .

— *Waddington (1977, p. 103)*

In real life, although some human problems may continue at a steady level of severity, many difficulties do not stay the same for long, but tend to increase and escalate if no solution or a wrong solution is attempted—and especially if more of a wrong solution is applied.

— *Watzlawick et al. (1974, p. 34)*

First there is only one possible, permitted, reasonable, logical solution, and if this solution has not yet produced the desired effect, apply it more forcefully. Second, under no circumstances doubt the assumption that there is only one solution; only its application may be questioned and "refined."

— *Watzlawick (1983, p. 33)*

One of the most influential ideas in the field of brief therapy has been the notion advanced by the Brief Therapy Center in Palo Alto that, under certain circumstances, problems develop from, and are maintained by the way that particular, and often quite normal, life difficulties become perceived and subsequently tackled (Watzlawick et al., 1974; Weakland et al., 1974). Guided by reason, logic, tradition, or "common sense," various attempted solutions are applied (which can sometimes include underreaction and denial), which either have little or no effect or, alternatively, can exacerbate the situation. A problem then becomes entrenched as *more of the same* solutions, or classes of solutions, become followed by *more of the same* problem, attracting *more of the same* attempted solutions, etc. A vicious cycle develops and the continued application of "wrong" or inappropriate solutions that lock the difficulty into a self-reinforcing, self-maintaining pattern can be seen as becoming the problem. Chronicity is seen as the persistence of a difficulty that is being repeatedly mishandled. As Weakland et al. comment,

> We assume that once a difficulty begins to be seen as a "problem," the continuation, and often the exacerbation, of this problem results from the creation of a positive feedback loop, most often centering around those very behaviors of the individuals in the system that are intended to resolve the difficulty. (1974, p. 149)

A similar situation can also occur in therapy as "more of the same" therapeutic approach leads to "more of the same" problem, and so on. Therapists can become quickly committed to a particular diagnosis and a particular approach, especially once they have made an emotional investment in how a situation *is* or how it *should* be. A diagnosis can thus become reified such that, even in the face of no change, the same therapeutic approaches will be continually applied such that "more of the same" will tend to lead to "more of the same," etc. For most professionals, when therapy becomes stuck, their training leads them to look harder and harder at the individual or family. This approach suggests that the opposite is as important, if not more so. When stuck, the therapist should look to their exploratory frameworks and at the approaches they are using, which may be "correct," but that are not working and may have become part of the problem.

Clearly, it is not always easy to persuade people to stop applying or even to reverse their attempted solutions, to try less of the same. This is not only because those solutions are guided by reason, logic, tradition, or "common sense," but also because they are often associated with and prompted by strong emotions that have been evoked by the problem and/or person(s) involved in the problem. They are also solutions that have worked at other times and in other circumstances ("That's how my parents dealt with me when I stepped out of line, and it never did me any harm!"). The more one invests both intellectually and emotionally in a particular position, the harder it tends to become to relinquish that position. However, as long as people feel respected and that their concerns have been heard and validated, it is our experience that they are frequently prepared, albeit sometimes cautiously, to attempt to stop doing what is quite clearly not working for them—to do less of the same. They often accept that this will, at the very least, save them much wasted time and effort, but also that it might, of itself, promote something new (in fact, this is often the case and quite frequently *is* the solution). After all, who knows what will move in to fill the considerable gap that is left?

A woman asked for a therapist's help so that she could help her husband stop drinking. He was a lawyer whose practice was beginning to suffer the effects of his frequently being drunk from midday onwards. She was constantly drawing his attention to the amount he was drinking, to the dangers of his driving home at night in such an inebriated state, to the way that his practice was beginning to suffer, to the way he was rarely home before the children went to bed. She would telephone him several times each day to check up on him. During the afternoons and early evenings, she would intercept his business calls to hide from his clients and colleagues the extent to which he had been drinking. He usually arrived home late and would often fly into a rage if any mention was made of the time or of the extent to which he had been drinking. She was increasingly avoiding social invitations because of the embarrassment she would feel because of his drunken behavior. She had become fed up with having to apologize to their friends for his behavior.

The woman was carefully asked whether any of these approaches had influenced her husband's drinking. It appeared that, if anything, the situation had become worse.

The woman was then given a copy of a handout that Brian

frequently gives to people to help them work out for themselves what it is that they might be doing that has become fruitless, however correct, logical, or justifiable it seems to be.

Approaches That Usually Do Not Work

The approaches outlined below, though they may be effective on an occasional basis (enough perhaps to keep us hooked), tend, when part of a chronic, regular pattern, not only *not to work*, but often to intensify the occurrence of the very behavior or attitude we are trying to change.

These approaches or positions tend to fail, not because people operate them poorly or with insufficient subtlety, nor because they have the wrong motivation. They appear not to work because they *just do not work*, however well you present your case and however logical or correct your case may be. In the same way that a ball that is released will always fall downwards not upwards, it is a "law" of human nature not to want, or be able, to cooperate in the face of the constant use of the following approaches.

A. The unsolicited lecture

- lectures ⎫ (especially when given
- advice ⎬ "for your own good!")
- nagging
- hints
- encouragement; "Why don't you just try to . . . "
- begging/pleading/trying to justify your position
- appeals to logic or to common sense
- pamphlets/newspaper articles strategically left lying around, or read out
- the silent, long-suffering "look at how patiently and bravely I am not saying or noticing anything" approach, or an angry version of the same (these are often the most powerful "lectures" of the lot)
- repeated and/or escalating punishments tend also

not to work and often result in more of the same, or
an escalation of, problem behaviors

B. Taking the high moral ground

when any of the above is operated from a position of
superiority, of "unassailable" logic (usually the male position), of moral outrage, or of righteous indignation; for
example:

"If you really loved me . . . "
"Surely you could see that if you . . . "
"Why can't you realize that . . . "
"Anyone with any sense . . . "
"After all I've done . . . "
"Look how ill/desperate/depressed I've made myself by
     worrying about . . . "
"I'll love you and stop being angry/walking out/refusing
     to speak, if you do exactly what I want."
"I love you because you behave as I want you to and
     will for as long as you remain that way."

any position, in fact, that implies that the speaker is in
possession of the truth about how things *are* or how they
should be, or has superior knowledge, abilities, or a set of
morals in which the other, by definition, is quite clearly
deficient or lacking

C. Self sacrifice/denial

- continually operating in order to keep the peace
- constantly "walking on eggshells" in order not to upset or to anger others
- constantly putting the happiness of others before
  your own
- continually seeking to justify yourself
- protecting others from consequences of their actions

- putting your own life permanently on hold: hanging on hoping the other will change
- continually trying to please somebody/everybody

D. Do it spontaneously!

where one person, through any of the above approaches, tries to make another do something or adopt a different attitude, but demands also that they should do it because they *want* to do it.

"You ought to want to please me!"
"I would like you to show more affection, but I'll only accept it if you do it because you want to!"
"It's not enough that you help with the washing-up, I would prefer you to do it gladly/willingly."

Trying to make somebody more responsible, more expressive, more reasonable, more thoughtful, more considerate, more sexy, more assertive, etc., is an invitation for them to be obedient to your definitions of how they should be, regardless of your actual intentions. It rarely, if ever, works. The best you will get is obedience; by far the most likely response will be an increasing inability to respond, disobedience, anger, withdrawal, failure, resentment. It appears that *most people do not like to be obedient.*

The implications of the ideas outlined in the above handout were discussed at length with the woman. She agreed that doing more of the same was unlikely to work and said that she was prepared to try something different. She decided to stop making her regular phone calls to her husband and also to stop protecting him by intercepting his business calls. She also decided to stop making any reference to his drinking, to the risks of his driving home in a drunken state, or to the time he arrived home. She decided to ignore his frequent tantrums rather than trying to calm him down. She also decided to begin to accept social invitations and to leave her husband to deal with the consequences of his behavior were he to become drunk and make a fool of himself. She would begin doing these things without announcing that she was going to be behaving differently in the future. (In our experience, it is usually better not to announce that there are going to be a new set of rules in a relationship but just to begin behaving *as if* the new rules have already been made.) At the same time, she realized that it was important that she do these things *not* to take the pressure off him, and not as yet another set of tactics to try to persuade him to moderate his drinking, but as a recognition that she needed to begin considering herself and that, ultimately, his liver had to be his own responsibility, however much she might remain concerned about him. She accepted that it would not always be easy to break the pattern of overresponsibility in which she had become stuck.

At the next session, she reported with considerable surprise that her husband had started, quite spontaneously, to come home earlier more regularly. He was now telephoning when he was going to be late, and had become much more attentive. After one of his temper tantrums, which she had apparently calmly ignored "in the same way one would with a young child," for the first time ever he had spontaneously apologized to her. His tendency to fly into a rage had subsequently decreased markedly. Several weeks later, he expressed to her his concern that he was drinking too much and that it was beginning to affect his business. She successfully resisted hitting the high moral ground (e.g., "That's what I've been trying to tell you . . . ") and responded, "It sounds as if you are really worried about this. I hope you can find a way of tackling it. If there is anything I can do to help, please let me know."

The woman was aware that, had she responded in the way she would earlier have done by becoming over-helpful, by encouraging him to see a therapist, arranging an appointment, etc., he would probably have begun struggling again with her rather than with *his* problem of *his* drinking. A couple of weeks later, he had sought out a therapist for himself.

Of course, the approaches outlined in the above handout are approaches that we all use in our therapy as well as regularly in our own personal lives. Every now and again we catch ourselves giving a client or family an unsolicited lecture from a position of "unassailable" logic on the general futility of giving somebody an unsolicited lecture from a position of "unassailable" logic. These approaches are not easy to avoid and, in certain areas of our work (for example where we have statutory responsibilities and particularly where we encounter family violence, rape or the sexual abuse of children), almost impossible. Nevertheless, in our experience, they continue to remain *approaches that usually do not work*.

When considering problems in terms of attempted solutions having become the problem, it is important to be clear over the issue of blame and responsibility. In no way was it seen by the therapist, or presented to the woman, that her attempted solutions were the reason for her husband's drinking. Care must always be taken that such an inference is not somehow inadvertently conveyed (bearing in mind that the information we intend to send is not always the information that is received). There have been arguments put forward that interactional explanations for problems infer, for example, that a woman is implicated in, and therefore must take a share in the blame for, the violence that her husband may have inflicted upon her. For example, McGregor comments,

> By working with the notion of complementarity, and giving focus to the psychological experience of the man and the woman, the violence is implicitly conceptualized as a relationship issue. Both parties are asked to describe what happens "between them and around them" when the violence occurs; thus the victim is implicated in the violence. By focusing on the female's "nagging" . . . there is a risk of implicitly reducing the violence to a level of annoying behavior, and a covert link may be made between female provocation (or nagging) and male violence. (1990, p. 69)

The fact that, on a particular occasion, had a woman not nagged she might not have been hit does not, in our view, mean that she is therefore responsible for the fact that a man deals with certain situations by becoming violent. However, we would see it as perfectly valid to help such a woman see how "nagging" has become an approach that does not work and how it has not helped her achieve what she wants (however valid her reasons may be for being angry with him) and thus persuading her to do less of it and trying something different. The fact that this may lead to her being bashed less often seems to us a positive outcome, though it may, by no means, necessarily be the resolution to the wider problem of her being in a relationship in which a man sees himself as having the right to be violent. If one of us tells a joke that makes another person laugh, we are clearly involved in stimulating that laughter though we are *in no way* responsible for whether or not that other person has a well-developed sense of humour.

The following is a more detailed example of encouraging "less of the same" as a way of tackling a potentially serious escalation between a young adolescent girl and her parents. Again, the approach taken is in no way intended to infer that the parents were to blame for the behavior of the daughter.

FREEDOM FOR WHOM?

Melissa was brought by her parents at the suggestion of a school counselor. A petite and pretty 14-year-old, Melissa sat sullenly while they described the deterioration in her behavior, both at home and at school, over the last year or so. A recent crisis had been precipitated by her staying out all night. This was, apparently, not the first time she had done this. She was often out until very late, frequented nightclubs, regularly drank alcohol, and it was suspected that she had smoked marijuana. Her academic performance had deteriorated markedly over the previous few months.

As the mother, Leanne, described the growing resentment and defiance they had been experiencing from Melissa, the father, Ron, sat looking angry, yet bewildered and defeated. Occasionally he would try to reason with Melissa, to ask her what was wrong, what did she want from them? All she would answer was, "I want more freedom," Ron would reply that she already had lots of freedom, but that the freedom she seemed to want was for a license to run wild and to do just what she wanted, regardless of how much it affected other people.

Melissa: "No I don't."
Ron: "Of course you do."
M: "I don't."
R: "What about these so-called friends of yours? They just seem to run wild around the streets half the night, and do whatever they want to do."
M: "They don't."
R: "They do. I know they do."
M: "They don't."
R: "As far as I can tell, that's what you're asking us to let you do."
M: "I'm not."
R: "So what *do* you want?"
M: "I just want more freedom."

At this point, defeated, Ron seemed to give up, turned to the therapist and said, "You see, this is it: She doesn't seem to want to be part of the family anymore."

To which Melissa replied, "I do."

Leanne described how difficult it was now to get Melissa to do her homework, how she gave no help in the home, how she was unpleasant to her two younger sisters, and, a point of particular concern to the parents, how she often would not come straight home from school ("It's not much to ask of her."). She would hang around with groups of friends, "loitering" at the bus station or down at the beach, often for several hours. In fact, the most recent crisis had occurred when Melissa had telephoned home about 8:00 p.m., having not yet come home from school, to be told furiously by Leanne, "Either you get yourself home here by 8:30, or don't bother to come home at all." She had finally arrived home at about noon on the following day.

With symmetrical escalations such as this, it is normally a good policy first to conduct a short family interview during which it is usually possible to develop a sense of how the members operate and then split the two factions up, the adolescent being seen alone first, and then the parents. Both sides are told that all such sessions are totally confidential and that information will not be carried from one side to the other, although what they themselves decide to share with each other later is, of course, up to them. This enables the therapist ethically to go into an overt coalition with each side in order to help them deal more productively with the difficulties they are experiencing in relation to the other side. From that point onwards, they would rarely be seen together again. Siblings, unless they also are involved directly in an escalation with their parents, are usually thanked for their help and offered no further appointments. The parents and the siblings would never be seen together *without* the "problem" adolescent present, particularly if those siblings seem regularly to side with the parents against their brother or sister. In this way, it is much easier to address, effectively and respectfully, the "attempted solutions" that each side is applying ineffectually to their perceived problems with the other side. The more the parents attempt to control, protect, help, or guide the adolescent, the more the adolescent is driven to retreat or rebel. The more the adolescent tries to "find space" by avoiding, by arguing with, or by disobeying their "over-intrusive" parents (as they see them), the more they confirm their parent's doubts and fears and thus attract further attention from them.

On her own, Melissa became much more communicative. She complained that her parents treated her as though she were an 11-year-old. Her mother was continually telling her when to change her clothes, when to shower, when to do her homework, how to organize her room, to come straight home from school, etc. Her father treated her as though she could not look after herself, "They say they want to trust me, but they won't give me the freedom so that I can prove to them that I can be trusted."

When asked by the therapist, "If you were me, what would you want me to advise your parents to do?" (most adolescents, in our experience, usually come up with perfectly sound and reasonable ideas when asked this question), she said she would advise them to back off, to give her more credit for being able to look after herself and to make sensible choices in her life. She confirmed that, if they were to cease their almost constant attempts to run her life for her, she would probably be much more cooperative with them.

She was told that the therapist would do what he could, but that he could not promise anything. He also added that he thought, given the reputation for teenage drug abuse and prostitution in the neighborhoods she tended to frequent, he might find it impossible to stop them worrying. She agreed that they were right to be worried about her when she was out very late at night and admitted that she often hated it and was "scared stiff" about the possibilities of being mugged or raped. However, the *certainty* that her parents would be waiting furiously for her when she arrived home usually outweighed, at the time, those more dangerous *possibilities*.

The parents were asked to describe in detail all of the ways they had tried to deal with the difficulties Melissa had posed for them. They had tried most of the things that parents do, berating her (sometimes in front of her friends), withholding privileges, preventing her from going out, reasoning with her, appealing to her, threatening her, etc. Recently, Leanne had sat for two hours at the bottom of Melissa's bed begging her to tell her what was wrong, asking her why she was doing these things. None of these approaches had made any difference.

The therapist commented that all of their approaches seemed to have become totally predictable to Melissa, such that she probably knew everything they were going to say by heart. It was explained that adolescents seemed to have a specially developed skill of closing their ears and glazing over their eyes whenever they detect that a predicable argument, lecture, appeal, etc., was in the offing. However, it was agreed that her staying out late was extremely worrying, particularly considering the areas she was frequenting, and that she certainly needed to learn to be more responsible. However, all of their attempts seemed at the moment to be getting them nowhere: "Yes, we know," said Ron, "But we can't just give her total freedom to do anything she wants."

The therapist empathized with the difficulty but commented that it seemed, in spite of all their attempts to get her
to change, she actually *was* doing more or less anything she
wanted. Did they feel that if they were to continue trying these
approaches that eventually they would get through to her?
Both parents agreed that this seemed unlikely, going on the
past record.

"So you basically have no guarantee, whatever you try, short
of chaining her up, which, of course, will only postpone the
problem, that she will not be staying out all night again some-
time during the next week?"

Both parents agreed that they had no such guarantee. At
this point in the interview, it seemed that they not only felt
understood and appreciated fully in their concerns, but also
that they had realized that a continuation of the approaches
they had so far been trying was unlikely to have any apprecia-
ble effect, however logical those approaches were. Only at this
point was it possible to ask them to try a rather radical experiment. They both agreed that they would be prepared to try
anything within reason.

It was suggested that, for the next week, they should totally
reverse their normal approach. It seemed that they were being
given a total runaround by their daughter, and the therapist
expressed that he felt that this should not be the case. It would
not hurt her to be thrown into a healthy level of confusion,
such that she was unable to predict how they would respond
to her at any point. This way, they could test how she would
respond when forced totally to take responsibility for her own
actions. They should avoid mentioning anything about the
time she finally came home from school, about where she had
been, when she should change her clothes, tidy up her room,
take a shower, do her homework, whether she should take her
meals with the family, etc. They should ignore totally all that
they, until recently, had been constantly tackling her about.

They were advised to ignore "quietly rather than noisily"
(i.e., just to ignore her behaviors rather than give a pained and

strained nonverbal message, "Look how we are ignoring you," such that it would still be clear to her that her behaviors were preoccupying them). They should, as far as possible, be warmly accepting of and civil to her. It was important to remember that they were ignoring certain of her behaviors, not ignoring *her*. If she were to come home at dawn, it was suggested that they ask her, as nonchalantly as possible, whether she'd had a pleasant evening and whether she would like a warm cup of coffee. It was explained that the therapist could not guarantee how she would respond to this change of response, and that he was painfully aware that he did not know where the next rapist was waiting to strike. However, he was sure that a continuation of what had recently been happening between them was almost guaranteed to escalate the problem further. They both agreed that this was probably the case, and said that they were prepared to give the suggestion "a good go."

When the family returned the following week, the therapist started off by seeing Melissa on her own. She reported that things were a lot better at home. Her parents were treating her with much more respect and had really "got off my back about everything." She said that there had been no "incidents" over the last week, but that this was partly because her parents had become much more flexible about the time she was to come home. She had not been more than half an hour later than any negotiated time ("Ten minutes late, before, and they used to bust me for it."). Interestingly, she said that she had not made any particular attempts to change her behavior or her attitude, it was just that things were much calmer at home.

Leanne described the changes in Melissa as "dramatic." Ron defined her as "noticeably different. . . . We had to bite our tongues at times, which was particularly hard the first time she was late home."

The therapist congratulated them, since, for the changes to have been *that* significant, they must have carried out their part of the experiment extremely well. ("I knew at the time I was asking a lot of you.")

Ron expressed a degree of caution about whether the changes would last. They were cautioned that adolescents will

always find a host of ways of inviting parents back into unpro-
ductive escalations that will render them impotent, and leave
the adolescents feeling misunderstood and victimized. The importance was emphasized of the couple working together to
avoid such a pattern reemerging. ("It's time you looked after
yourselves for a change.")

Apparently, other people had also commented on how Melissa's attitude had changed, how much happier she seemed, how
much less defiant she had become. Her grandmother had noticed how much more a part of the family she had suddenly
become. The couple were encouraged to continue doing more
of what was obviously beginning to work.

The following appointment, set for three weeks later, was
canceled because Leanne was unwell. As things were still going well, it was left that they should make contact if they felt
a further session would be necessary.

Two years later, a follow-up telephone call confirmed that,
although they had been through a range of what Leanne described as "normal teenage hiccups," the situation had remained dramatically different, with no repeat of the earlier difficulties.

"We have learned now when to stand our ground, and when to
avoid fruitless battles about issues over which basically we
have little control, things that Melissa really has to sort out for
herself. She's much more responsible nowadays. Now that we've
stopped worrying so much about her, and arguing over her,
Ron and I are getting on so much better."

8

EXCEPTIONS, SOLUTIONS, AND THE FUTURE FOCUS

The self isn't in the memory, only the story we believe about ourself. It can also be revised. It's constantly being revised. We see what it was we did, and we make up a story to account for it, and believe the story, and think that we understand ourself.

— Orson Scott Card (1987, p. 179)

The re-appraisal of past acts and the appearance of surprise in present acts gives men indeterminate futures.

— Strauss (1977, p. 33)

In recent years a new resource-oriented philosophy of approaching human problems has emerged in the field of psychotherapy. This philosophy builds upon openness and cooperation focusing on what is positive — on strengths, progress, and solutions. The application of this philosophy is not restricted to psychotherapy; it appears to be relevant across the entire spectrum of the helping services.

— Furman & Ahola (1992, p. 162)

Brief therapists work from the assumption that people have many areas of competence upon which to draw in order to surmount difficulties. Even in the area of what is defined as a problem, it is assumed that there are times when people are less pressured by the problem or that they deal with it more effectively, or with some of its various manifestations. However, these differences in coping ability tend to be forgotten or discounted in a client's or family's sense of being unable to solve a problem, or sometimes in their inability to believe that it can be solved or modified or, at least, made more bearable. In this chapter we will consider some of the approaches and techniques that have become subsumed under the general heading of "solution-focused" (de Shazer, 1985, 1988, 1991; de Shazer et al., 1986; Furman & Ahola, 1992; Walter & Peller, 1992) or "solution-oriented" (O'Hanlon & Weiner-Davis, 1989).

In our opinion, the work of Steve de Shazer and his colleagues at the Brief Family Therapy Center in Milwaukee has represented one of the most interesting developments in the field of brief therapy over this last decade. While many seem to have become concerned with building elaborate theoretical castles, often based on the works of varied anthropologists, physicists, and biologists, de Shazer and his colleagues have continued to work towards clearer and more precise descriptions and definitions of the essence of effective therapy.

In 1984, de Shazer and Molnar described four specific interventions that they were beginning to use regularly. In particular, they introduced what was to become a routine first-session task, given to clients, couples, or families regardless of the problem with which they presented.

> "Between now and the next time we meet, we(I) want you to observe, so that you can tell us(me) next time, what happens in your (life, marriage, family, or relationship) that you want to continue to have happen." (1984, p. 298)

They found that, in many cases, concrete and significant changes occurred between the giving of this task and the following session.

> With surprising frequency (50 of 56 in a follow-up survey), most clients notice things they want to have continue and many (45 of the 50) describe at least one of these as "new or different." Thus, things are on the way to solution; concrete, observable changes have happened. (de Shazer et al., 1986, p. 217)

The efficacy of this formula intervention was empirically tested by Adams et al. who found that the first-session task "was an effective intervention in the initial stages of treatment for gaining family compliance, increasing the clarity of treatment goals, and initiating improvement in the present problem" (1991, p. 288). Though they pointed out that they were not seeking in their research to comment on the overall effectiveness of the solution-focused model, they expressed some doubts about the first-session task's effectiveness in increasing family optimism about treatment outcome.

In *Keys to Solution in Brief Therapy* (de Shazer, 1985), the idea was advanced that solutions are not necessarily as closely related as it may seem to the problems that they address. A number of "formula interventions" were elaborated through which, it was argued, the process of developing solutions could be started. It was suggested that this could be done without the necessity of knowing very much about the nature of the problem to be solved. The analogy of a skeleton key was invoked. With such a key many doors can be opened without the need to find the one correct key that fits the exact shape of the lock.

Weiner-Davis et al. highlighted the extent to which significant changes frequently seemed to occur prior to the first appointment. They began to ask the following question:

Many times people notice in between the time they make the appointment for therapy and the first session that things already seem different. What have you noticed about your situation? (1987, p. 306)

Molnar and de Shazer elaborated a list of formula interventions that were beginning to be used in addition to the "first-session task":

1. Client is asked to do more of the behaviors which are satisfactory and different from the problem behavior.
2. Client is asked to: "Pay attention to what you do when you overcome the temptation or urge to . . . (perform the symptom or some behavior associated with the symptom)."
3. Client is given a prediction assessment such as whether in the time between sessions there will be more instances of behavior that are an exception to the problem behavior.
4. Client is told "Between now and the next time I(we) would

like you to do something different and then tell me(us) what
happened."

5. Client is asked to do a structured task (such as keeping a
   log of certain incidents) which is related to those times when
   the problem behavior ceases or is not present.

6. Client is told: "The situation is very (complicated, volatile,
   etc.). Between now and the next time, attempt to identify
   why the situation is not worse." (Molnar & de Shazer, 1987,
   p. 355)

The common theme with all of these interventions is their
concentration on things that are working or beginning to work,
rather than on an exploration, clarification, or categorization
of pathology.

In his next book, *Clues: Investigating Solutions in Brief
Therapy*, de Shazer further summarized the basic principles
behind the solution-focused approach, highlighting the importance of exceptions, and also introducing the technique of the
"miracle question" in which clients are invited to describe the
specific differences they or others would notice if the problem
was suddenly and mysteriously solved overnight (1988).

EXCEPTIONS

Central to the solution-focused approach is the certitude
that, in a person's life, there are invariably exceptions to the
behaviors, ideas, feelings, and interactions that are, or can be,
associated with the problem. There are times when a difficult
adolescent is *not* defiant, when a depressed person feels *less*
sad, when a shy person *is* able to socialize, when an obsessive
person *is* able to relax, when a troubled couple *resolves* rather
than escalates a conflict, when a bulimic *resists* the urge to
binge, when a child does *not* have a tantrum when asked to go
to bed, when an overresponsible person *does* say no, when a
problem-drinker *does* contain their drinking to within a sensible limit, etc. These exceptions are also usually associated with
other differences in behaviors, ideas, feelings, and interactions
that are happening at the same time. Yet, as de Shazer observes,

Problems are seen to maintain themselves simply because they maintain themselves and because clients depict the problem as *always happening.* Therefore, times when the complaint is absent are dismissed as trivial by the client or even remain completely unseen, hidden from the client's view. Nothing is actually hidden, but although these exceptions are open to view, they are not seen by the client as differences that make a difference. (1991, p. 58)

A man who was, by his own admission, extremely overprotective of his 21-year-old son, such that he would telephone him several times each day, finally decided he would take a two-week holiday with his wife, giving no forwarding address or contact telephone number to any of their three grown-up children. He was encouraged by the therapist in his resolve not to telephone home for the whole fortnight, though it was acknowledged that this might be rather difficult. At the next appointment, three weeks later, the man abjectly announced that he had failed. Asked to elaborate, he admitted that, on the seventh day, he had finally given in to the urge to telephone "to check up on how things were." He had spoken to the "problem" son who, to his surprise, had reassured him that things were fine (which they subsequently found out had been so) and that there had been no need to check up on him. The man appeared quite depressed by his "failure."

The therapist asked, "But what about the 13 days on which you didn't telephone? That must have been extremely difficult to resist at times, but nevertheless, it appears that you succeeded."

As the man considered this achievement, his demeanor began to change. Eventually he admitted, "You know, I'm not really very good at recognizing my accomplishments. I haven't had a lot of practice at it. But I think you are right. That holiday really *was* a success."

In this approach, clients are invited to recognize and then to build on what *they are already doing* that can be defined as successful or, at least, as heading in the general direction of dealing more effectively with the problem. Clearly, to be persuaded to consider these "successes" it is important that the

client or family experiences the therapist as hearing, as understanding, and as validating the felt experiences of failure,
anger, distress, depression, etc., that are their usual responses
to the problem. The extent to which a recognition of the existence of exceptions can become the springboard from which
further changes can occur is directly related to the extent to
which those exceptions are, or can be made, meaningful to the
client or family.

Clearly, it would be easy to highlight exceptions in such a
way that the client or family feels patronized, or feels that the
therapist really does not understand the seriousness of their
problem, or the distress, guilt, anger, etc., that it has caused
them. Thus, it is important that the therapist avoid becoming
over-preoccupied that a client or family *must* recognize the
existence of a particular exception, or avoid entering into an
argument with them about its significance. As John Weakland
has said (personal communication), "Never argue with a client."
It is often much better to maintain a puzzled skepticism rather
than a crusading zeal.

> "I am *still* puzzled as to how you managed to avoid, this time,
> becoming caught up in your usual angry response pattern? It
> can't have been easy. Most people would have lost their temper
> within the first few seconds."

> "Yes, I know that it must seem a small thing, but your daughter
> really does sound as if she could try the patience of a saint. I
> can't see your halo, so you clearly aren't a saint. So, how the
> hell did you resist wringing her neck last night?"

> "From what you have told me, I think *I* would have become
> depressed. How on earth did you manage to keep going and to
> get on with doing what you had to?"

It is often useful to ask people questions such as, "How did
you manage to do that?" Such questions not only highlight
success, or degrees of success, but can also help elicit contin-
gencies in people's lives that are, and can be highlighted as,
associated with more successful functioning:

"I was able to keep going because I knew my husband was supporting me, this time."

As we touched on in Chapter 4, it can be most affirming for people when the difficulty of their situation is attested to by questions such as, "Given what you have told me about your situation, I am really surprised that things are not much worse. How have you kept going?"

As Miller comments, "By asking how a client has been able to make some progress, or maintain or prevent their problems from becoming worse, the therapist and client are able to review situations that appeared to be failures as solutions that simply went unnoticed" (Miller, 1992, p. 7).

When people are talking about their perceptions of their problems, the therapist can most usefully aid the process of deconstructing a negative, problem-focused view by being not too quick to understand.

> Client: I know I've got some problems. I'm over sensitive. I'm basically a noncompassionate person. I don't make friends easy.
>
> Therapist: Where did you get these ideas from, that you're somehow noncompassionate . . . ?
>
> Cl: Well I guess . . . I know you've got to feel me out. I know . . .
>
> Th: Were you shooting a line when you said you're worried about your wife? That sounds like compassion. I'm a bit puzzled.
>
> Cl: Well . . . how can I be noncompassionate *and* oversensitive?
>
> Th: Yes.

de Shazer has commented,

> perhaps the best that therapists can do is creatively misunderstand what clients say so that the more useful, more beneficial meanings of their words are the ones chosen. Thus, creative misunderstanding allows the therapist and the client to to-

gether construct a reality that is more satisfactory to the client. (1991, p. 69)

In his most recent book, *Putting Difference to Work*, de Shazer describes a brilliant example of this from the work of Insoo Kim Berg (de Shazer, 1991, pp. 63–67). Berg was consulted by a woman describing herself as a nymphomaniac. She found herself unable to go to sleep unless she had had sex at least once that day. She was in no way prepared to accept those nights that she had been able somehow to restrain herself as meaningful exceptions, nor to see learning to restrain herself from sex as a viable solution. For her, this would mean her marriage was bad. At one point, the husband, who saw himself as becoming a stud rather than the lover he would prefer to be, commented,

> Husband: But for me, it's more of a sleep problem for both of us.
> Therapist: I wonder about that. Maybe we've been looking at this the wrong way.
> Wife: Do you have any cures for insomnia?
> Therapist: I don't know. We've been looking at this as a sex disturbance, but it's beginning to look more like a sleep disturbance. (de Shazer, 1991, pp. 64–65)

Described as a problem of insomnia, the difficulty was apparently rapidly resolved. The issue of nymphomania was never again addressed. The woman described both her sleep pattern and her libido as having "returned to normal." Clearly, the success of this therapy was related directly to the extent to which the alternative definition made sense to the woman. In this approach, the question of which was objectively the "real" problem becomes irrelevant. In the process of negotiating what it was that was being addressed in the therapy, the therapist's somewhat puzzled approach led to the potentially more intractable problem of nymphomania (the woman considered that it was rooted in infancy and would require deep therapy) becoming deconstructed to be replaced by the more easily addressed problem of insomnia. Each "problem" had sufficient behavioral and emotional overlaps that could be highlighted such that *either* could become a legitimate area of focus (bearing in mind that such legitimacy must exist, ultimately, in the eye of the beholder, in this case the woman, rather than in the mind of the therapist).

THE MIRACLE QUESTION

A powerful way of helping people to focus on potential solutions rather than on problems is the miracle question.

"Suppose that one night there is a miracle and while you are sleeping the problem that brought you to therapy is solved: How would you know? What would be different? What will you notice different the next morning that will tell you that there has been a miracle? What will your spouse notice?" (de Shazer, 1991, p. 113)

As de Shazer goes on to say, "Clients frequently are able to construct answers to this 'miracle question' quite concisely and specifically" (p. 113). The actual process of how the problem will be solved, and thus many of the client's attendant doubts, can thus be bypassed. He is also at pains to attribute the genesis of this idea to Milton Erickson and his use of pseudo-orientation in time as a hypnotic technique.

These ideas are utilized to create a therapy situation in which the patient could respond effectively psychologically to desired therapeutic goals as *actualities already achieved.*
   This was done by employing hypnosis and using, conversely to age regression, a technique of orientation into the future. Thus, the patient was enabled to achieve a detached, dissociated, objective and yet subjective view of *what he believed at the moment he had already accomplished*, without awareness that those accomplishments were the expression in fan-

tasy of his hopes and desires. [emphasis added] (Erickson, 1954, p. 261)

The client, the couple, or the family members are encouraged to imagine, in as concrete a way as possible, what the many differences will be. We often ask them to imagine what specifically would be seen or heard as noticeably different if a videotape recording were to be made of them on the following day. It is important that the therapist be gently persistent in his or her eliciting of a clear and specific behavioral description. We are not seeking a fuzzy picture of some future dream, Utopian or otherwise. As O'Hanlon and Weiner-Davis assert, "It appears that the mere act of constructing a vision of the solution acts as a catalyst for bringing it about" (1989, p. 106). The process of gathering this information can take a considerable time and should not be rushed.

People usually find it much easier to describe how *other* people should be different (particularly the spouse with whom they are having marital difficulties, or their problem child). This can tend to perpetuate more of the same "high moral ground," "why can't you see what you are doing wrong," stance that will often be insufficiently different to their usual interactions around the problem. It is better that they be encouraged to describe what the differences will be in their *own* behaviors and attitudes, what they will notice about themselves. Ultimately, people can only change themselves. It can be particularly useful for them to consider what differences other people, such as their spouse, children, friends, work associates, or strangers will notice in their behaviors and attitudes.

"What will you be doing or saying differently such that other people will know you are less depressed?"

"If you were in a restaurant and people were watching the two of you having a meal together, how will they know that you are getting on well?"

As the Scottish poet Robert Burns so eloquently expressed it in "To a Louse,"

> O wad some Pow'r the giftie gie us
> To see oursels as others see us!
> It wad frae mony a blunder free us,
> And foolish notion.

When people describe the differences in terms of an *absence* of either a behavior pattern or an emotional state, it is useful to ask them what it is that they will be doing or feeling *instead*. Ultimately, it is easier to engage in a clearly defined alternative action than it is just to resist doing something without having some other behavior to take its place, particularly if it has become a deeply entrenched habit. Descriptions of changes in feelings are best translated into descriptions of specific behaviors that will be clear evidence to others that their mood has changed.

Client: I won't be sitting around feeling sorry for myself all the time.

Therapist: What will you be doing instead?

Cl: I'll be happier.

Th: What will you be doing such that other people will know that you are happier?

Cl: I will be smiling more often.

Th: What else?

Cl: I will start making contact with my friends again. I've lost contact with most of them.

Th: What will *they* notice different about you?

Cl: Well, first of all they'll notice that I am actually making contact with them. (Laughs)

Th: What else will they notice?

Cl: That I'm interested in going places again. I used to go out to eat a lot. A whole group of us used to. I suppose they still do. And I used to go to a lot of concerts.

Th: So you'll be doing that again?

Cl: Yes.

Th: What differences are these changes going to make to you?

Cl: I will have a sense of direction in my life, again.

Another way of focusing on the future is to ask a question such as, "If, when you come back next week, you are telling me that your problem has improved significantly, what is it that you will be telling me about?" or, when talking to a couple, "What will be the differences in you that your partner will be telling me about?" Another approach is, "If I pulled out a magic wand and were able to perform magic on your situation, what will be happening that is different from before?" (O'Hanlon & Weiner-Davis, 1989, p. 106).

Important in the exploration of how things will be different is the therapist's careful use of language that presupposes the inevitability of change. The word "when" is used rather than "if"; "What else *will* be different?" is asked rather than "What else *would* be different?" "*When* things begin to improve . . . " is asked rather than "*If* things begin to improve. . . . " "*As* you become less inhibited . . . " is asked rather than "*If* you were to become less inhibited. . . . " "*When* you stop hearing voices . . . " rather than "*If* you were to stop hearing voices. . . . "

Once a clear picture of what people think will be different has been elicited, it then becomes possible to find ways of encouraging or enabling people to experiment with new behaviors. de Shazer describes asking a couple secretly to choose, without discussing it with the other, two days over the following week during which they are to pretend that the miracle they have elaborated has actually happened. They are then to observe how the other reacts to them. They are also each to try to guess which two days the other has chosen, but to keep it to themselves until the next session (de Shazer, 1991, p. 144). On this occasion, the behaviors were left unspecified by the therapist. Where it is clear that a couple or a family have different goals, or the therapist is unsure, it is important to be unspecific and refer generally to "the problems that bring you here." Where people are obviously in agreement over goals, it is possible to ask them to practice specified behaviors on their chosen "miracle" days.

A young woman had been able to construct quite a long list

of specific things she would start doing again following such a miracle. She was invited to toss a coin each day.

"Each time the coin comes up heads, I would like you to do at least two of the things on your list. You can do more, of course, but I'm only asking you to aim for two. On the days when the coin comes up tails, there is no pressure on you. You are free to decide yourself what you will do on those days."

Clearly, people will usually only follow such suggestions if the behaviors they are being asked to try out are consistent with their ideas about how they want to be, rather than how the therapist or some other person wants them to be. The important thing about inviting people to practice specific behaviors is that, as Kiesler has shown, when people engage in particular patterns of behavior that are associated with, or promoted by, particular beliefs or attitudes then their commitments to those beliefs or attitudes becomes confirmed or strengthened much more quickly and profoundly than if they just talk about them (Kiesler, 1971).

SCALING QUESTIONS

Another effective way of focusing on achievement and solution is through the use of scaling questions, which can be used in a variety of ways.

"On a scale ranging from zero to ten where zero represents things at their worst, and ten represents how things will be when these problems are resolved, where would you place yourself today?"

As Kowalski and Kral point out,

the scale builds on an assumption of change in the desired direction. Since a scale is a progression, the number "7" assumes the numbers "10" as well as "5," "3," or "1." It assumes movement (change) in one direction or another, rather than stagnation. By

> virtue of this, an expectation of change is built into the process
> of asking scaling questions . . . since the use of a scale enhances
> a suggestion of change in either the desired or dreaded direc-
> tion, it also implies a degree of control on the part of the client
> for navigating the direction . . . the business of goal setting is
> accomplished, since the poles and the area between the problem
> and the goal are made quantifiable and objectifiable. (1989, p. 61)

Such scales can be used to consider a whole range of aspects
of a client's life. In fact, there is no experience that we can
think of that cannot, in some way, be looked at through the
lens of a scaling question.

> scaling questions can be used to assess the client's self-esteem,
> self-confidence, investment in change, willingness to work hard
> to bring about desired changes, prioritizing of problems to be
> solved, perception of hopefulness, evaluation of progress, and
> so on — things considered too abstract to concretize. (Berg, 1991,
> p. 88)

To explore fully the many ways that this technique can be
used would take a whole chapter. We will confine ourselves
here to giving a few examples from which the reader should be
able to infer or invent many of the other ways in which it
might be used. We will be using a scale of zero to ten in our
examples. However, any other scale can be used. For example,
if smaller gradations are deemed necessary (e.g., where very
small, cautious, incremental changes are being discussed or
suggested), a scale of zero to one hundred could be used. When
working with couples, particularly where there seems to be
some question over the motivation of one or both, we have
found the following question useful in opening up a debate
that can often help a couple begin to look more productively
at their relationship.

> "If zero represents 'I couldn't really give a damn' and ten repre-
> sents 'I'm really enthusiastic,' where would each of you place
> yourself today in respect of working on your relationship?" or
> "Where do you think your partner would place him/herself?"

If both scale their motivation as low, it is possible to ask what will have happened were they to return to the following appointment to announce that they had both moved up a point or two. Similarly, if there is a discrepancy, the partner giving the lower number can be asked a similar question. Alternatively, the miracle question can be used to explore similar themes.

It is also possible to explore the extent to which people view the likelihood of change.

"If zero means you believe you are basically going to be like this for the rest of your life and ten means that there is a good chance that you'll have this problem beat at some point in the future, where would you place yourself on that scale today? What would it take for you to move up half a point or even one point on the scale?"

It is important when enquiring about movements up the scale that the therapist choose realistic gradations erring on the side of the conservative rather than the over-optimistic. If the client is experiencing a higher degree of optimism, it is better that he or she has to persuade the therapist about that. If the therapist pushes too quickly for change, such that the client feels pressured, he or she is more likely to adopt the "yes, but" position. As suggested above, in some situations, a scale of zero to one hundred might be less threatening in that smaller gradations can be used.

Looking at a client's progress through the medium of a scale can often give him or her a different perspective on how things are going. A young woman, during her fourth therapy session, was still expressing many negatives about how her life was progressing, in spite of the various "exceptions" that the therapist had been highlighting (which were clearly, at that stage, more meaningful to him than to her). About half-way through the session she was asked,

"If zero represents how you felt when you first came to see me and ten how you will see yourself at the end of therapy, where would you put yourself at this point?"

After a few moments thought, she described herself as being somewhere between four and five.

> Therapist: So you are beginning to get somewhere near
>   to approaching half-way?
> Client: Yes.

For the rest of the session, as the specific events and behaviors that represented this improvement were elaborated (the therapist being careful to follow the process with caution and restraint rather than to push as enthusiastically as he had been earlier), the woman became increasingly more optimistic about her situation.

> "If, by the next session, you have finally managed to reach five, the half-way mark, what are the new things you are going to tell me about?"

A young man, who apologetically admitted that he felt he'd only reached three on the scale, was surprised and encouraged when it was pointed out to him that he was "almost a third of the way there."

Scaling questions can also be used with young children as well as with adults. Words are, of course, not the only medium we can use. We can draw charts, or ask the child to draw them. There are many creative ways that young children can be helped to depict where they feel they are in respect of the dimension we are exploring with them.

> "If this single brick stands for when you are being very noisy in class and behaving like a five-year-old, and this tall pile of bricks stands for when you have been able to behave like a ten-year-old, what size of pile would stand for how grown-up you have been these last few days?"
>
> "If this small circle on the blackboard shows me how shy you used to be, and this big circle shows me how brave you are going to be, draw me a circle to show me the bravest you have been this week."

THE FUTURE-FOCUS

*Since all the world is but a story, it were well for thee to buy the
more enduring story than the story that is less enduring.*

— *St. Columbia of Scotland*

We all live in our past, our present and our future. As we
have suggested earlier, our perception of all of these is a highly
selective one. The future exists in our anticipation of how it
will be. Traditionally, therapies have concerned themselves
with the past and with the present, with attempting to effect
changes in them through a process of reexamination. What is
new and exciting in the field is that it appears that the future
is *also* open for reexamination, even though it has not yet
happened. Furman and Ahola have summarized this move toward a future-focus as follows,

Since the future is often connected to the past, people with a
stressful past are prone to have a hopeless view of their future.
In its turn a negative vision of the future exacerbates current
problems by casting a pessimistic shadow over both past and
present.

Fortunately, the converse is also true; a positive view of the
future invites hope, and hope in its turn helps to cope with
current hardships, to recognize signs indicating the possibility
of change, to view the past as an ordeal rather than a misery,
and to provide the inspiration for generating solutions. (1992,
p. 91)

9

FRAMING INTERVENTIONS: ALTERING HOW THE PROBLEM IS VIEWED

Nothing is good or bad except thinking makes it so.

— Hamlet, *William Shakespeare*

Bateson is generally given the credit for invoking the term "frame" to indicate the organization of interaction such that at any given time certain events are more likely to occur and certain interpretations of what is going on are more likely to be made.

— *Coyne (1985, p. 338)*

As a thing is viewed, so it appears.

— *The Tibetan Book of the Great Liberation*

Our symbolic thought process imposes upon us the categories of "either-or." It confronts us always with either this or that, or a mixture of this and that. . . . In the realm of experience, nothing is either this or that. There is always at least one more alternative, and often an unlimited number of them.

— *Zukav (1979, p. 284)*

To reframe, then, means to change the conceptual and/or emotional setting or viewpoint in relation to which a situation is experienced and to place it in another frame which fits the "facts" of the same concrete situation equally well or even better, and thereby changes its entire meaning.

— *Watzlawick et al. (1974, p. 95)*

In Chapter 3, in discussing the nature of reality, we introduced the important distinction to be drawn between facts and meanings.

THINGS or EVENTS are limited to sensory-based observations and descriptions; what is actually there, what is happening, or has happened, that can be perceived by our senses.

MEANINGS are interpretations, conclusions, and attributions that are derived from or related to the facts of the matter.

The behaviors and associated emotions (or *vice versa*) that lead people to seek therapy are a reflection not of "things or facts" but of the meanings that are attributed to them. We have suggested that people are constantly engaged in drawing distinctions as they seek to make sense of their world and that they develop frameworks or hierarchies of constructs that, in large measure, determine how they will make sense of and thus respond to their experiences. It is these "frames" that are, in our view, the major focus of therapy, since changes can only occur where alternate meanings become available such that different responses can be made to subsequent experiences. As de Bono has asserted,

> A frame of reference is a context provided by the current arrangement of information. It is the direction of development implied by this arrangement. One cannot break out of this frame of reference by working from within it. It may be necessary to jump out, and if the jump is successful then the frame of reference is itself altered. (de Bono, 1971, p. 240)

There are basically two approaches to helping people "jump out" of the frames that can be seen as limiting their ability to take a different perspective on and thus begin to resolve problem situations.

If the therapist provides or encourages the development of a new or alternative frame or meaning to a situation (either directly or indirectly), this is called *reframing*.

For example, Lorraine, aged 17, was brought to therapy by her mother. A rather pretty, slightly overweight young woman, she kept her head bowed during much of the interview, looking out from beneath her hair. The therapist was told that, over the last few months, she had become depressed and introverted, and was now becoming increasingly anxious about starting the new school term, which was to commence the following week. Lorraine had herself asked to see somebody about these problems. When asked, she agreed with what her mother had said. The therapist asked,

> Therapist: What was it that decided you to come to see somebody now?
> Mother: Well, she says. . . . Do you want to tell him, Lorraine?
> Lorraine: No, you can explain it.
> Mother: She says that she feels different from all the other girls. She finds that she cannot relate to them at all. She has lost touch with all of her old friends.
> Therapist: Different in what way?
> Mother: Is it alright, Lorraine, if I tell him about what has happened?
> Lorraine: Yes, it's OK.
> Mother: Well, Lorraine was sexually abused by her father a number of times up until about a year or so ago. She went to see some counselors then, which helped a bit, but I think that she is still being affected by the experience. She has a very low self-esteem.
> Lorraine: When I look at the other girls at school, I know that I am not like them. I am abnormal.

After enquiring further, in some detail, about Lorraine's beliefs about how the experience of the abuse was affecting her, the therapist commented, "It seems to me, Lorraine, after talking to you, that you are actually quite normal. It's the thing that has happened to you that is abnormal, not you. You are a normal person trying to deal with an abnormal experience."

From this point, Lorraine's demeanour changed dramatically. Subsequent feedback from both Lorraine and from her mother proved that the drawing of this distinction had represented an important turning point for her. It created a new frame from which she was able, almost immediately, to begin to see herself more positively. She successfully negotiated the return to school and encountered no problems in reintegrating with her friends.

If the therapist challenges (again, either directly or indirectly) the meanings that the client associates with the situation without providing a new frame, this is called *deframing*. The client can be left to create or discover alternate meanings for themselves or can be left without any particular meanings. For example, the following is a brief excerpt from a therapy session:

Client: I know what my faults are, OK, but I've had them for 46 years.
Therapist: And do you think you're kind of stuck with them?
Cl: I'm stuck with them. There's no way you're going to get rid of my faults.
Th: A lot of people think that.
Cl: Well, maybe I will.

Reframing and deframing are not two discrete techniques. As the above examples demonstrate, to reframe requires that something is deframed, just as to deframe clearly means that something is potentially reframed. The reframing about normality will have deframed the young woman's view of her abnormality; the deframing of a belief in the impossibility of changing the habits of a lifetime, will have reframed the client's view of the potential of therapy. The difference between the two is essentially a matter of focus.

We would propose reframing to be the most basic and necessary operation in the process of change. Everything else is subordinate and either aids or, alternatively, impedes this process, or can be seen as the trimmings that reflect any particular therapist's beliefs and prejudices about therapy and the nature of change (not necessarily unhelpful in their therapy but sometimes unhelpful in the development of theoretical clarity).

A recent paper has questioned the extent to which, in their use of framing techniques, brief therapists have tended to ignore the "subjective truths" of their clients or families. Also questioned is the extent to which framings are imposed upon people rather than developed out of a collaborative process (Flaskas, 1992).

The apparently cavalier, manipulative, "anything goes" approach that brief therapists are alleged to use in selecting "truths" when reframing, exists, in our experience, largely in the minds of certain commentators, as does the alleged lack of interaction apparently involved in the development of these frames. Any good brief therapist knows that no frame will be of any help unless it makes more than just intellectual sense to a client or family, and frames are not pulled out of the air (at least, not by good brief therapists) but guided by direct information often painstakingly gained from the client or family through the process of the interview and therefore involving the members' "subjective truths." It is not that brief therapists have no respect for people's personal experience of "truth," far from it, but that we believe, in human interactions, that there are many potential "truths," some that seem to inhibit change and others that seem to promote it.

> the determinants of the level at which an activity is framed and how this may be altered. . . . Preliminary experiments suggest that when an action can be framed at both a higher level ("having a boring life") and a lower lever ("watching television all afternoon"), there will be a tendency for the highest level framing to become prepotent, with the lower level framing ignored. (1985, p. 339)

However, as he goes on to quote from the work of social psychologists Wegner et al., when people come to think about the *details* of their action, they become particularly impressionable about the overall meaning of what they are doing. A new understanding of the action can emerge, and this understanding can then lead to the development of a new action. (Wegner et al., in Coyne, 1985, p. 340, emphasis added)

The potency and the healing potential of reframing appears to stem from the fact that it is often not possible for us clearly to "know" what it is that underlies our tendencies to engage repeatedly in particular actions or continually to play a particular role in our interactions.

As for the question of who produces the frame in brief therapy (or, we would argue, in any effective therapy), it must surely be an interactional process in which the therapist is sensitive not only to behavioral phenomena (even though they may be a major focus of enquiry) but also to the explanations (true, for them) that the family members hold about the problem, and the affective experiences elicited (real, for them) both by their views of the problem and also by the process of the therapy. However, the therapist's suggestions about different ways of framing situations are central in that they arise from an outside perspective. By definition, clients (as do all of us) tend to think about their situation through the frames they customarily use, frames that will, in part, be blinding them to alternatives. The harder we look through a pair of blue-tinted spectacles, the more we will see the world colored blue. Sometimes, particularly where we have forgotten we are wearing those spectacles and thus have ceased to question the validity of our senses, we need somebody to lend us a pair of a different hue. We surely all have had the experience of introspecting about problems and often spiraling to the most pessimistic conclusions and embedding ourselves even more deeply and hopelessly into them. The fact that the therapist's input (or offer of the loan of a pair of spectacles of a different hue) suggests a new way of considering things does not mean that the client or family has thus become the helpless recipient of manipulation.

We agree with Flaskas (1992) that clients (as do we all) retain some (we would say considerable) commitment to, and interest in, judging their own experiences and understandings of truth. We believe that any approach to therapy is capable of ignoring this, the brief approaches no more nor less than others. Believing in the absence of any absolute "truth" is not synonymous with ignoring or riding roughshod over the "subjective truths" of others. The usefulness of any "truths" used in the proposing of different frames for a client's or family's consideration rests primarily on how these frames are viewed from the subjective perspectives of those involved (influenced profoundly as they will be by their own beliefs and their affective responses both to the frame and to their experience of the therapist). To do this helpfully and respectfully clearly means listening at all times with profound levels of care and attention to what family members are saying.

A young unmarried mother, who had been deserted during her pregnancy by the man she had loved, brought her nine-year-old son to see a therapist. She reported that, whenever she brought home a male friend, the son would behave atrociously, swearing, sometimes behaving aggressively towards the man, and refusing to leave them alone. She had become afraid to take anyone home. The son was also described as being close to his grandmother who lived nearby and who remained, according to the woman, overprotective towards her daughter, tending to disapprove of her various men friends. Toward the end of the first session, the boy was described by the therapist as extremely sensitive and aware of his mother's underlying fear of becoming emotionally involved again and of being hurt, in the way that his father had hurt her. He was also aware of his grandmother's concern for her daughter and so, perhaps partly on behalf of his grandmother but particularly because of his own love for his mother, he seemed to have decided to protect her from her own emotional vulnerability. Therefore his apparently "bad" behaviors were an attempt to be helpful by both protecting her from becoming overinvolved and by giving her an outlet for her own tension and anxiety through anger at him. Only a man who truly loved her would be prepared to tolerate what the boy was doing. The therapist solemnly commended the boy for his concern and recommended he continue to care for his mother.

At the next session the mother reported vast improvements in her son's behavior. At a follow-up several months later, she confirmed that the improvements had continued and that she was now much more comfortable about bringing people home. In fact the boy had already become quite friendly with her most recent man friend.

As we have earlier commented, it is clearly important that a new framework be sufficiently congruent with a family's, couple's, or individual's experiences, even though it introduces a different way of viewing those experiences. If there is insufficient congruence the frame will usually be rejected or denied. It is important also to remember, as Coyne cautions, "Reframes sometimes grip patients in the artificiality of the therapy session . . . only to be invalidated in their first encounters with their everyday environments. It is useful to assume that reframes have not taken hold until patients have acted upon them and validated them *away from therapy*" [emphasis added] (1985, p. 342).

A sensitive reframing will often touch feelings and thoughts that until then have remained hidden and it may be these that give power to the "new" frame. In the above example, the therapist's acknowledgment of the extent to which the mother had been hurt by the desertion all those years ago and feared the possibility of being hurt in that way again, may well have been a crucial element.

A reframing will almost inevitably place a positive connotation on behavior normally viewed within the client's or family's belief system (and often that of the therapist/observer) in a more negative way. In the following example, though positive connotation is used, there is also a concealed challenge to both members of the family, delivered by the therapist, not in an overtly challenging way, but with an attitude of benevolent concern.

A widow who had successfully brought up two daughters, both of them now married, was having problems with a 15-year-old son who was mixing with the "wrong sort" and also was involved in glue-sniffing. It seemed that the mother was over-concerned about the boy and giving him little opportunity to mature and separate. At the end of the first session an opinion was expressed to both mother and son, but addressed primarily to the mother, as follows:

> "You have obviously been a good mother to your daughters but, without a husband's support, it has been difficult for you to fully understand your son. This must have been a great worry to you. James is now 15 years of age. There is a point in adolescence when all young men suddenly grow out of many of their childish traits and begin to act like more grown up men. With some this process takes longer than others. However, it is usually at about this age.
>
> "I am sure James cares for you and worries what will happen to you when he finally leaves home, but doesn't know how to make you feel less isolated. This he will find easier when he begins to leave his childishness behind and begins to move towards manliness. Most glue sniffers tend to be boys who are nervous of moving towards manliness and are scared to get involved in more serious and mature activities such as studying and courtship.
>
> "I am convinced that you are not the sort of mother who wants to keep her son a baby, tied to her apron strings. You would be surprised how many single mothers try to turn their sons into substitute husbands.
>
> "I suggest that you watch James closely for the next two weeks to keep a close check on how much of his childishness is still around, but also be prepared to recognize the first signs of approaching adulthood, however slight. I feel that it is important to insist that James not cheat and try to act like a man before he is ready for it, although, as I said, with most boys it begins to happen at around his age. When he becomes a man, it is important that he is a *real* man and not the sort of boy that has to act tough or become delinquent in order to cover up his scaredness."

During the delivery of this opinion the boy's expression was a study of concentration, in marked contrast to his earlier tendency to grin and ignore what was being said. From this point the boy's behavior began to improve. His mother changed her perception of him and became less demanding and overpowering. Two sessions later she came without the boy, giving no explanation. She used the session to talk with the therapist about her own problems of loneliness and insecurity.

A couple were arguing constantly over the behavior of their "out of control" children and particularly over what was the appropriate way to discipline them. The therapist pointed out that their arguments spoke highly of their determination to "get it right" and that it was clear neither of them would be satisfied until they were sure they had found the correct approach, one that both of them could agree on. He further suggested that, uncomfortable though it was for them, it might be necessary to continue to argue, even perhaps to redouble their efforts, until they were convinced they had reached a satisfactory resolution. The parents looked at each other with what appeared to be warmth and increased respect and agreed to what the therapist had suggested. Over the next few weeks, they argued much less and became much more consistent in their handling of the children (whose behavior, perhaps predictably, improved).

There are many ways "correctly" to have labeled this couple's apparent inability to work together either as evidence of marital disharmony or as evidence of the existence of pathology, in either or both, in one of the many ways that such pathology can be identified (readers are referred to *DSM* whatever-number-it-is-up-to for an elaboration of many of these). Labeling their arguments as evidence of good intentions seemed to invoke a higher level framing (e.g., "We share a wish to be good parents.") that perhaps allowed for and enabled a change in the interpretations of behaviors (e.g., "We are fighting basically because we agree.") and thus in behaviors themselves.

A woman executive sought therapy because she lost her voice (it became very hoarse and shaky) when she spoke in meetings. She initially stated that it was related to "low self-esteem." When asked how she knew this difficulty was related to her speaking difficulty, she seemed somewhat surprised and mentioned that she had been to a hypnotist who suggested that they work on her self-esteem as a way of getting over the problem. The therapist replied, after gathering more information, that as far as he could tell, there was no connection between her self-esteem and this voice difficulty. Furthermore, with the evidence she had provided, in addition to her appearance and demeanor (she was well-dressed and spoke articulately and confidently), he saw little evidence of a lack of self-esteem. On the contrary, she seemed to have a good level of self-esteem. He asked if she felt badly about herself. She replied that, no, she did not, but had assumed this was a problem after seeing the hypnotist (with no results) and reading many self-help books. It was suggested that the present therapy concentrate on matters more relevant to her current concerns about speaking more successfully in meetings. She readily agreed.

This represents a good example of deframing. The causal attribution that her difficulties were related to a hypothetical entity, "low self-esteem," was respectfully and successfully challenged. She was relieved instantly of a pathology such that the possibility of a rapid resolution of her difficulty was made much more likely.

We have found that, at times, a reframing can be more powerful if it comes from someone other than the therapist, as in the following example (this example dates from a period when Brian was still experimenting with Milan style reframings).

A visiting therapist was asked to act as a consultant for a team that had become stuck in their work with a particular family. The parents had sought help with a 13-year-old girl, the oldest of three children from the wife's first marriage. Also involved in the therapy was the wife's mother, in whose house the family was living. The girl was troublesome both at home and in school, was involved with a gang of adolescents that was often in trouble, and was described as a compulsive liar.

The consultant, watching from behind a screen felt strongly

that the mother and grandmother, while in many ways clearly close, were, at the same time, extremely competitive, particularly over who was the "best mother" to the girl.

The family had been informed that the therapist had asked a consultant to join the team on the other side of the screen because she felt stuck and unable to help them at the present time. At the end of the session the family was told that the therapist would be receiving a report and that she would be in contact about further appointments at a later stage.

Within a few days the husband was sent a copy of the consultant's report and asked to read it to the whole family at the earliest opportunity. In her letter the therapist stated that, though the report was intended to help her, she was sending a copy to them because she felt the family to be one that thought seriously about their problems.

The report read as follows:

It is obvious to me that this is a close family and one that wishes to stay close. I strongly feel that Jane is an extremely sensitive girl and that she quite obviously very much loves both her mother and her grandmother (and they obviously love her, however exasperated they might get at times with each other). But, for reasons that I do not yet fully understand, Jane seems to experience a sense of divided loyalty, which may be why she acts in such an unhappy way.

It seems that she worries about all of them, but for some reason she seems particularly worried about her mother and grandmother, although both of them may find this hard to believe, as a child's "worried" behavior often comes out like "naughty" behavior.

It may be that Jane, deep down at the back of her mind (though she will not be aware of this and might obviously deny it), takes too seriously to heart some of the differences between her mother and grandmother and worries that one of them may become ill or depressed if the other "wins" what Jane seems to see as an emotional battle between them. (It's as if she feels there's a competition as to who is the best mother of the two of them.)

I feel it is important to point out to the family that it was quite obvious that [the grandmother's family] are a close family, though maybe difficult for outsiders to get close to, and that I feel strongly that every member is concerned with remaining close even though sometimes they may seem to behave in the opposite way. Thus it will not always be easy for the family to recognize, under surface behaviors, how loving and concerned Jane is.

At the next session, three weeks later, the family reported the girl's behavior as being much improved. In fact, she had been no trouble since the previous session.

As with any technique, this one is, of course, no panacea. We have given examples of several reframings or deframings that have been particularly effective, sufficient in themselves to bring about significant changes. Although, with hindsight, successful interventions appear obvious and relatively simple, our experience is that finding the "right" framing is often a complex task requiring considerable sensitivity, empathy, creativity and, at times, courage. We have many examples of ineffective reframings that have had little or no effect and about which we have decided not to write. However, our experience of "getting it wrong" is that the worst that usually happens is that the family or client rejects or denies the proposed frame, and so we go back to the drawing board.

10

PATTERN INTERVENTION: ALTERING THE DOING OF THE PROBLEM

Therapy is often a matter of tipping the first domino.

— Milton Erickson, *Rossi, 1980, vol. 4, p. 454*

When you have a patient with some senseless phobia, sympathize with it, and somehow or other, get them to violate that phobia.

— Milton Erickson, *Zeig, 1980, p. 253*

. . . maladies, whether psychogenic or organic, followed definite patterns of some sort, particularly in the field of psychogenic disorders; that a disruption of this pattern could be a most therapeutic measure; and that it often mattered little how small the disruption was, if introduced early enough. . . .

— *Rossi, 1980, vol. 4, p. 254*

Brief therapists often seek to resolve presenting complaints in therapy by altering the patterns of action and interaction involved with and surrounding these complaints. They seek to integrate individual and interactional approaches through the unifying notion of altering the context of the presenting complaint. By altering these patterns with their regularities and redundancies without references to causal, functional, or other explanatory hypotheses, presenting complaints can often be briefly and successfully resolved.

Individual and interpersonal approaches are often viewed as being at odds with one another. One is either a "systemic" therapist or an "individual, linear" therapist. We, however, find no conflict between the two. The unifying concept of pattern can be used to bridge the (apparent) gap. What the two approaches have in common is the discovery and alteration of patterns of thought and action surrounding a complaint. If causal, functional, and other explanatory hypotheses are avoided, no conflict need arise. How and why the patterns came to be, what function or meaning they have and other such speculations are viewed as irrelevant and distracting to the main task; that of discerning the patterns of thinking, action, and interaction surrounding and arguably maintaining the complaint, and helping the client alter them. In this chapter we will look at some ways that it is possible to intervene into such patterns.

Automatic patterns of action, of interaction are necessary and desirable aspects of life. They help people to organize experience, perceptions, and behavior and to improve efficiency in behavior. In many of the normal aspects of day-to-day life, patterns or regular ways of doing things enable us to function without having to renegotiate relationships and meanings every time. For therapy purposes, it is only necessary to alter automatic patterns when they contain or accompany undesired experiences or behaviors (symptoms). To intervene into a pattern is to replace any element in the pattern with one falling outside the customary limits, to remove or to add elements.

"For example, at a certain point in a binge-eating pattern, a person may take a taste of some cake, or cookies, or bread, or ice cream, or chocolate (but never carrots, celery, cottage cheese, or hard-boiled eggs), and then go on a binge including all of the former items but none of the latter (i.e., if they eat 'forbidden,' 'fat,' or 'nondiet' foods they typically or always binge, and they never binge on 'good,' 'nonfattening' foods). This is followed by self-induced vomiting in the toilet, or in the sink, or in the bath (but never in the garbage can, or in a bucket, or on the carpet). And in terms of the circumstances surrounding this part of the sequence, the initial taste may be taken standing up or walking around (but never sitting or lying down), the binge-eating may take place in the kitchen, or in the dining room (but never in the bedroom or in the backyard), in the middle of the night or in mid-afternoon (but never first thing in the morning or just before bed), always alone (and never with other people around), and usually while doing nothing else in particular or sometimes watching TV (but never while talking on the telephone or feeding the cat and dog). The pattern will have a different range—with different elements—for each person, so it is not possible to come up with some fixed 'catalog' of ranges or elements or of interventions. For example, many binge-eaters binge only when alone, but some binge with others around occasionally or frequently. One needs to find out the limits of the class of things that would serve equally well to maintain the pattern as still being this particular person's binge pattern" (O'Hanlon, 1987, pp. 34–35).

Some may avoid going out with friends on the days when they have been bingeing. Other binge-eaters might never get dressed on the days on which they binge. Although not directly involved in the bingeing, altering these accompanying regular patterns might bring about an alteration in the complaint context that would lead to the resolution of the presenting complaint. There can be a wide range of alternative behaviors that will maintain a binge-eating pattern. As with music, there will often be countless variations on a theme that can be played such that the basic underlying theme remains the same. What needs to be introduced are some variations outside that range, variations that can introduce a new theme. In a new and unfamiliar pattern, all sorts of unexpected things can happen.

In asking questions about the pattern around a complaint, not only do we ask, "When does it always occur and when does it never occur?" or "Is it always X, or is it ever Y?" but also we ask hypothetical questions such as, "When would it always occur, and when would it never occur?" and "Would it always be X, or could it ever be Y?" Moreover, we often "help the client out" by suggesting possible alternatives ourselves. Since clients are often unaware of what the pattern is, they frequently say, "Well, there's no particular pattern to it" or "It could be just about anything," but careful questioning never fails to reveal regularities with fairly distinct limits.

> It must be remembered that patterns are not "things." However, they are the next best thing to "things." They are descriptive abstractions. When observing some actions, an observer can abstract *patterns* of actions. This does not involve theorizing or explaining the existence of these facts, speculating about what function they serve, or other forms of "psychologizing." It is more like classifying organisms into species or objects into a set. (O'Hanlon, 1987, p. 52)

While the patterns abstracted are abstracted by an observer, it is our contention that they are based on observable facts and therefore are different "animals" from those "inventities" of psychology such as "ego deficits," "low self-esteem," or "a need to punish oneself."

PATTERN INTERVENTION

Once the therapist has gathered specific sensory-based information on the pattern and the range of the pattern, she or he sets about (in conjunction with the client) finding ways of helping the client alter the pattern. Milton Erickson stressed in his work the importance of utilizing aspects of the client's own behavior and beliefs. For example,

a. The patient's language
b. The patient's interests and motivations
c. The patient's beliefs and frames of reference
d. The patient's behavior
e. The patient's symptom(s)
f. The patient's resistance (O'Hanlon, 1987, p. 24)

Frequently the easiest and most straightforward way to intervene in a context containing a complaint is to encourage the client(s) to alter the performance of the complaint in some small or insignificant way. The work of Milton Erickson contains many examples of this type of contextual intervention. Erickson might direct a compulsive handwasher to change the brand of soap with which he or she usually washes. He might ask a person who smokes to put the cigarettes in the attic and the matches in the basement. He once instructed a thumb-sucker to suck her thumb for a set period of time every day. He directed a couple who constantly argued about who was to drive home after a party (at which they'd both had a few drinks) that one was to drive from the party until they were just one block from home. They were then to stop the car, switch places and the other was to drive the rest of the way.

An alteration of the performance of the complaint changes the patterns around it and often the complaint (either gradually or abruptly) disappears. The therapist may accomplish this alteration using direct or indirect approaches, with authority or in a cooperative venture with the client. Different strategies will suit the style of different therapists.

O'Hanlon has outlined the following list of the main ways of intervening in a pattern.

1. Changing the frequency/rate of the symptom/symptom-pattern
2. Changing the duration of the symptom/symptom-pattern
3. Changing the time (of day/week/month/year) of the symptom/symptom-pattern
4. Changing the location (in the body or in the world) of the symptom/symptom-pattern
5. Changing the intensity of the symptom/symptom-pattern
6. Changing some other quality or circumstance of the symptom
7. Changing the sequence (order) of events around the symptom
8. Creating a short-circuit in the sequence (i.e., a jump from the beginning of the sequence to the end)
9. Interrupting or otherwise preventing all or part of the sequence from occurring ("derailing")
10. Adding or subtracting (at least) one element to or from the sequence
11. Breaking up any previously whole element into smaller elements

12. Having the symptom performed without the symptom-pattern
13. Having the symptom-pattern performed minus the symptom
14. Reversing the pattern
15. Linking the occurrence of the symptom-pattern to another pattern – usually an undesired experience, an avoided activity, or a desirable but difficult-to-attain goal ("symptom-contingent task") (O'Hanlon, 1987, pp. 36–37)

Examples of Intervening to Interrupt Patterns

Milton Erickson told the following story,

A medically retired policeman told me, "I have emphysema, high blood pressure, and, as you can see, I am grossly overweight. I drink too much. I eat too much. I want a job but my emphysema and high blood pressure prevent that. I would like to cut down on my smoking. I'd like to get rid of it. I'd like to quit drinking about a fifth of whiskey a day and I'd like to eat sensibly."

I said, "Are you married?"

He said, "No, I'm a bachelor. I usually do my own cooking, but there's a handy little restaurant around the corner that I often visit."

"So, there's a handy little restaurant around the corner where you can dine. Where do you buy your cigarettes?"

He bought two cartons at a time. I said, "In other words, you buy cigarettes not for today but for the future. Now, since you do most of your own cooking, where do you shop?"

"Fortunately, there is a little grocery right around the corner. That's where I get my groceries and my cigarettes."

"Where do you get your liquor?"

"Fortunately, there is a nice liquor store right next to that grocery."

"So, you have a handy restaurant right around the corner, a handy grocery right around the corner, and a handy liquor store right around the corner. And you want to jog and you know you can't jog. Now, your problem is very simple. You want to jog but you can't. But you can walk. All right, buy your cigarettes one pack at a time. Walk across town to buy your pack. That will start to get you in shape. As for your groceries, don't shop at the handy grocery around the corner. Go to a grocery a half mile or a mile away and buy just enough for each meal. That means three nice walks a day. As for your liquor, you can drink all you want to. Take your first drink at a bar at least a mile away. If you want a second drink, find another bar at least a mile away. If you want a third, find another bar a mile away."

He looked at me with the greatest of anger. He swore at me. He left raging.

About a month later a new patient came in. He said, "A retired policeman referred me to you. He said you are the one psychiatrist who knows what he is doing."

The policeman couldn't buy a carton of cigarettes after that! And he knew that walking to the grocery was a conscious act. He had control of it. Now, I didn't take food away from him. I didn't take tobacco away. I didn't take liquor away. I gave him the opportunity to walk. (Rosen, 1982, pp. 149–150)

A 13-year-old girl was continually being checked up on by her elderly parents. She was seen as untrustworthy, aggressive, lazy, uncooperative, and unhelpful. Though the girl showed no motivation to be involved in therapy, she began to express interest when asked by the therapist whether she would be prepared to trick her parents. To this she readily agreed. She was asked to do a number of things over the next couple of weeks that she knew would definitely please her parents. However, she was to do them in such a way that they did not know what it was that she had done. Neither was she to let on, even if asked. She was to deny that she had done anything, even if they were to guess correctly.

The parents, meanwhile, were to make every possible attempt to find out what it was she had done and to keep a written list. They could discuss it together but were not allowed to ask her.

At the next session, the girl was seen separately. She admitted that she had not really made any efforts to do anything but admitted that things had been much better between her and her parents. When the parents were seen, they brought with them a long list of all the things that they had detected that they thought she had done in order to please them.

It seems that, whether the girl undertook her part of the suggestion or not, her normal behavior patterns contained sufficient nonconfrontative, cooperative acts, which perhaps were normally not noticed, to satisfy the parents that things were changing. From the daughter's point of view, the parents' constant vigilance, against which she was normally rebelling, had taken on a new meaning and become an attempt to discover evidence of good rather than bad behavior.

A 17-year-old retarded boy, recently placed in a school away from home, developed a habit in which he rapidly alternated his right arm out in front of him at a rate of 135 times per minute. Milton Erickson had the boy increase the rate to 145 times per minute. Over a course of some time, the rate was decreased, under Erickson's supervision, to 135 again, increased to 145, then decreased and increased by alternating an increase of five times per minute and a decrease of ten times per minute until the movement was eliminated (Rossi, 1980, vol. 4, pp. 158–160).

A bulimic woman reported that the very longest duration she had managed for a bingeing episode was one hour, was told that she must stretch the duration of bingeing (i.e., before vomiting) to two hours. She could increase this duration in any manner she wished.

A woman who was struggling to cut back on her drinking was advised that, for the time being, she should drink as much as she felt she wanted. It was pointed out that she was still struggling to recover from a difficult time she had been experiencing over the previous year. However, she agreed to remove all of her clothes in front of a full length mirror and to put them on back-to-front before pouring out a drink (apart from her shoes, which might have required her to dislocate her feet). She was then to return to the mirror, remove the clothes and put them back on the right way round before sitting down and enjoying her drink. If she decided that she wanted a second drink, she was to repeat the exercise. The same again if she decided she wanted a third, and so on. The exercise apparently caused her much amusement and, within a week, her drinking was under control.

A couple, who argued constantly and said they had trouble not falling into an argument even when both had the best intentions not to fight, was told (by a student of ours) that, as soon as they started to argue, they were to head for the bathroom where the husband was to remove his clothing and to lie down in the bathtub while his wife was to sit (fully clothed) on the toilet. They could then continue the argument.

A six-year-old thumb-sucker who only sucked his left thumb was seen by Milton Erickson. The boy was told that he was being unfair to his other digits, not giving them equal time. He was told to suck his right thumb, and eventually, each of his other fingers. Erickson remarked that as soon as the boy divided his thumb-sucking between his left and right thumb, he had in effect reduced his habit by fifty percent (Rossi et al., 1983, p. 117).

A couple sought therapy from Erickson for marital difficulties. They ran a small restaurant together and constantly quarreled about the best way to run it. The wife insisted that the husband should be in charge, as she'd rather stay home. However, she feared that, without her constant supervision, he would ruin the business, so she continued to work alongside her husband and they continued to quarrel. Erickson gave them this assignment: Each morning, the wife should see to it that her husband was to go to the restaurant half an hour before her. As they only had one car but lived only a few blocks away, she could walk there half an hour later. When the wife arrived, the husband had already successfully fulfilled many of her "irreplaceable" functions. She began coming in later and later each morning and leaving earlier and earlier before closing until finally she rarely showed up at the restaurant at all unless she needed to replace somebody who was away sick. The bickering ceased (Haley, 1973, pp. 225–226).

A lawyer who wanted to quit smoking agreed that if he smoked a cigarette he would do 15 minutes of the paperwork he had continually been putting off before he smoked any additional cigarettes.

A couple sought marital therapy, the main complaint being that the husband was a "work-a-holic" (both agreed on this point). The husband constantly broke his promises to be home on time, which led to bitter arguments almost every evening. He complained that his wife wanted him to spend his only day off visiting his or her parents. It was agreed that, instead of complaining, the wife would record the amount of time her husband was late during the week and he would have to visit his or her parents for that amount of time on his day off without complaining.

A woman who had been hospitalized several times for depression described how she was still spending much of her time unproductively worrying about anything and everything. Each day she was achieving very little. Her husband had tried everything he could to encourage her to become more active. She agreed to consider during the following week, before her next appointment, whether she would be prepared to agree to follow any instruction the therapist was to give her, without knowing in advance what was going to be asked of her. She was reassured that it would not be anything that would be beyond her nor would it harm her.

She returned to the next appointment agreeing, with determination but also with considerable trepidation, to accept the challenge. She was instructed that, on each day that she felt she had wasted too much of her time in fruitless worry (and only she, not her husband, was to be the judge of this), she was to retire to bed at the normal time but to set her alarm for 2:00 a.m. She was then meticulously to scrub the stone floor of the kitchen (they lived in a stone cottage in Wales) following which she was to do half an hour of typing practice (she had been trying unsuccessfully to teach herself to touch-type). Then she could return to bed. On any day that she felt she had been sufficiently productive and not wasted too much time in fruitless worry, naturally she would not have to follow this routine. The next session was fixed for two weeks time.

She returned to the next session announcing that she had only had to scrub the floor once (and she had cleaned it so thoroughly that she had felt surprisingly proud of her achievement). The rest of the fortnight had been the best she had experienced for a long time.

A prison officer brought his family in for therapy because of his concerns about his 15-year-old daughter who was continually fighting with both him and his wife. She was described as stubborn and deceitful, and they feared she was "becoming promiscuous." There were three other daughters, a 14-year-old (described as "a treasure"), and identical twins aged 12.

The father held extremely strict ideas about how families should be run. Family meetings would be convened whenever problems occurred. These would become extremely heated and would consist of accusations and counter-accusations, the elaboration of lists of "crimes" as well as the evidence for these crimes. The 15-year-old was invariably the "accused" in these meetings. The 14-year-old was careful not to take sides. As the family heatedly described their problem, the therapist felt as though she was being invited to act as judge.

The therapist suggested that, in future, the twins should be given the right to call a halt whenever a battle between their sister and either of the parents became too heated. The twins should immediately convene a family "court hearing." The 14-year-old was then to become advocate for the aggrieved parent and the other parent was to become advocate for the girl. The protagonists were not allowed to present their own case although they could, of course, brief their respective advocates in private; it would be the advocates who would be responsible for examining witnesses and presenting evidence. The case was to be heard by the twins who were to act as jury, note the evidence, and prepare a verdict, which was, however, to be kept a secret until delivered to the therapist at the following session.

The family seemed highly amused by this suggestion and agreed to try it. Two weeks later, they returned to describe how, at their one attempt at a "court hearing," they had all dissolved into fits of laughter. However, no major problems had actually occurred. They had enjoyed a harmonious two weeks. The hearing had been called over a rather trivial issue "just to see what it would be like."

Clearly, the success of interventions such as these are dependent on the rapport that can be built between the therapist and the client or the family. Also important is the issue of customership. Is the intervention targeting some aspect of the client's or family's life in which they are emotionally invested and also in which they have an investment that a solution be found? If this is not the case, clients will be unlikely to follow the suggestions and, thus, the patterns will remain unchanged.

11

THE USE OF ANALOGY

*We dream in metaphor, and at our deepest levels we dialogue in
metaphor, and through metaphor we can achieve fundamental
understanding.*

— Wallas (1985, p. 3)

A young couple in therapy was finding the open discussion
of a sexual problem extremely difficult and quickly shifted the
subject to another area of contention, the decorating of their
house. Describing how they went about the task, the wife explained with a slight expression of distaste, "I do the stripping,
he gets on with the job, then I have to clear the mess up after
him."

It would be possible to define this change of subject as resistance and attempt to refocus the couple onto their sex life. It
would also be possible to see the wife's statement as a metaphorical comment on how she had come to see the sex act as a
chore and attempt to help the couple see this connection, thus
refocusing the therapy back onto their sex life. Another approach would be to accept the couple's metaphor and discuss
with them possible resolutions to the problem surrounding the
decorating of their house. When successful, this approach can
lead the couple to the beginnings of a resolution of the sexual
problem without their necessarily being faced with it being
discussed (or perhaps, more likely, they will be aware of it at
one level, but choose to help create the myth that the discussion is about the decorating of houses). It is with the latter
approach that this chapter will concern itself.

ABOUT ANALOGY

Erickson and Rossi asserted that, "Analogy and metaphor as well as jokes can be understood as exerting their powerful effects through the . . . mechanism of activating unconscious association patterns and response tendencies that suddenly summate to present consciousness with an apparently 'new' datum or behavioral response" (Erickson et al., 1976, p. 226). Koestler has suggested that "the aesthetic satisfaction derived from metaphor, imagery and related techniques . . . depends on the emotive potential of the matrices which enter into the game" (1975, p. 321). In other words, the more evocative the associations produced by what is either denoted or connoted by an analogy, the greater the creative potential.

Any time one thing is likened to another or spoken of as if it were another thing, analogy is involved. "We seem to have reached a dead end in this discussion." "Your smile is like the summer sun." Such phrases are in common use and are, in fact, so common, we sometimes fail to recognize them as analogy. These devices are used to cast a different light on a subject. We know what a dead end is when we are traveling along a road, so we can understand the analogy when it is used to characterize a discussion. We have experienced a summer sun, so we can imagine that a smile that is likened to it would be bright. Analogy helps us use skills and understandings from one area of our experience to approach differently or to understand and make sense of other areas of our experience.

For example, Milton Erickson, in his treatment of a boy who wet his bed, used analogies to gain access to abilities the boy had developed in other contexts for him to use to solve his bedwetting. He discovered that the boy played baseball and proceeded to launch into a long discourse about the fine muscle control necessary to be a good baseball player. The outfielder must open his glove just at the right time and clamp down just at the right time. To throw the ball to the infield, he must release the ball just at the right time, too early or too late will cause the ball to go where he does not want it to go. Next, he told the boy about his digestive tract and how food goes into a chamber where muscles at either end close down for the proper amount of time, relaxing and releasing the food when it is time to move it to another chamber. He talked to the boy about archery, describing the complex coordination of the many muscles of the eye necessary effectively to aim an arrow. All these analogies had a common theme, that of the automatic control of muscles, just what the boy needed to use to stop wetting the bed.

The simplest and most basic analogies are those that cross-reference from one of the senses to another, a technique much used by poets; for example "a warm smile," "my heart is heavy," "a stony silence," or "his mood was black." Koestler observes that " . . . the emotive potentials of the sense-modalities – sight, sound, odour, touch – differ widely with different people" (1975, p. 321).

Grinder and Bandler (1981) refer to the therapeutic advantages of initially adopting a client's preferred mode. Careful attention paid to the kind of imagery used by people should soon indicate which is their preferred representational system. For example, a man might say, "I have spent years building up my life, now everything has come tumbling down, everything is in pieces, my life now looks hopeless." To respond to this man with something like "You felt empty, it seems everything feels heavy" or "The way I hear it, nothing sounds positive to you anymore," introduces different representational systems; the imagery does not match the man's mode of articulating his world as demonstrated by his choice of words.

Thus, a more congruent response to the man might be "You want to put your life back together again, you can see all the parts around you, but it's as if you've misplaced the repair manual, the bits don't seem to fit anymore." Grinder and Bandler suggest that people who come into therapy will tend often to have become stuck in one or another representational mode. They assert that simply introducing the other modes by gradually overlapping from their preferred mode can begin to effect internal changes. For example, with the above man, it might be possible to continue "It is as if you are sitting, surrounded by the bits of your life. To begin the work of reassembling them must feel a heavy burden; it must feel too much to carry on your own." The therapist has overlapped from the visual to the kinesthetic and the man may follow to explore his problem through different mental pathways, thus possibly making accessible a wider range of internal connections and association.

ANECDOTES, PARABLES, AND STORIES

Throughout history, anecdotes, parables, and stories have been used to teach, to embellish, to explain, to enrich, to encourage creative thinking, sometimes to puzzle. In such an approach, significant features of the storyline and facets of the relationships between the participants or components in the story should stand in a direct analogic correspondence to events and relationships of importance to the listener and to his or her circumstances.

Analogy can be used directly to amplify something that the therapist wishes to convey. For example, a woman arrived for marital therapy without her husband and complained that his "moodiness" made life with him very difficult. She despaired of any change in his personality ever being possible and occasionally despaired of the marriage. In the ensuing discussion, it was discovered that she was a horse trainer who was quite renowned for her ability to work with "untrainable" horses. She was challenged to think of her husband as a difficult horse (she suggested that he was a mule) and was asked how she would deal with such a situation. She quickly responded with a list of principles that she used with horses, such as be consistent, do not get angry with the horse, build on small changes, etc. She was able to see, with some coaching, how these principles could be applied to her "untrainable" husband.

Alternatively, analogy can be used more indirectly. The advantage of using anecdotes and stories in this way is that conscious mental "sets" can be bypassed.

For example, a woman, deserted many years ago by her husband, had struggled to raise two learning-disabled children, a boy and a girl, now teenagers about to leave school. She seemed to be finding it extremely difficult to tolerate any signs of independence in either of them, though she had complained endlessly to a succession of therapists that they would not grow up or act responsibly. It seemed that what this woman feared most of all was that, having sacrificed much of her life to bringing up her children, she would be deserted by them once they became independent. The family members were fond of animals and so, towards the end of a session, the therapist asked them for some advice. He told them that he had a cat who had given birth to two underdeveloped kittens. Now that they finally were strong enough and had been given away, she was inconsolable, spending hour after hour mewing, searching the house for them. What advice could they give him? The daughter quickly said, "Don't get rid of her." The mother said, "What she wants is lots of love and reassurance." When it was suggested that maybe the problem had something to do with the cat having had to work much harder than normal because of the kittens being weak, the mother commented, "Some of us mothers sometimes don't want to let go."

At the end of the subsequent session it was reported that, to his surprise, the therapist had not needed to do anything. One at a time the kittens, who had been given to local families, had returned to visit. As though reassured that they still loved her, his cat had now settled down; in fact, she would chase them away back to their own homes if they stayed too long. The son remarked, "So they found their own solution." Showing the family a photograph of the cat served to make the family more attentive to the unfolding story.

The use of this and other metaphors enabled the therapist to explore the fears of this mother, fears that she would be abandoned by her children, a topic she would deny and refuse to discuss if it was more openly broached. The analogy used suggested more optimistic futures in a way that would not easily be possible overtly. In this case, at no point was a connection made by the therapist between the anecdotes and the woman's own circumstances.

A single, 25-year-old woman, with three children by three different fathers, telephoned in considerable distress requesting an urgent appointment. Yet in therapy, though she had alluded briefly to having had an extremely difficult and traumatic childhood, she gave no sign of distress or any indication as to why she had requested an urgent appointment. The more the therapist sought clarification, the more calm and unruffled she appeared. The three children played quietly together on the floor.

Suddenly, he asked the children whether they knew the story of the ugly duckling. They had heard it at school. The therapist discussed with them at some length how the ugly duckling had been pushed from pillar to post, how *she* had thought that there was no place anywhere for *her*, how she had wished finally to die. As this discussion progressed, the woman began looking increasingly distressed then finally, in tears, she cried out, " . . . and I tried so hard to make this last relationship work!" The session continued as though they had been discussing her own experiences of insecurity and rejection rather than the ugly duckling. The fairy story had been sufficiently similar to her own traumatic experiences to trigger an affective response.

USING THE BODY'S NATURAL SKILLS

A woman sought therapy for persistent warts, which were mainly located on her hands. She had been to a dermatologist for 18 months on a regular basis to have the warts removed by freezing. This approach had painful after-effects, however, and the warts kept returning. She sought hypnosis, as she had heard that hypnosis could cure warts. After helping her into trance, the therapist told her about irrigation ditches used in Arizona to water the plants and how pipes were used to irrigate each crop row. When the pipe was removed from the row, the hot desert sun would wilt the weeds, which were more fragile than the crops. Just like that, he told her, her body knew how to regulate the blood flow and withdraw nutrients from the warts, but to still keep the skin alive. He gave her the task assignment of soaking her feet in the hottest water she could stand for 15 minutes followed by soaking them in the coldest water she could stand for another 15 minutes. Several other analogies were offered, like the process of blushing automatically and how the blood went to her digestive area after she ate a meal, etc. All these were to help her transfer her ability to alter her blood flow and thus eliminate the warts. Three sessions of this type of treatment were sufficient to clear up the warts, and regular follow-up of several years indicated no recurrence.

A man sought Milton Erickson's help for persistent pain in a leg that had been amputated. His wife also reported that she had tinnitus (ringing in the ears). Erickson began the session by telling the couple about a time during his college days when he had spent the night on the floor of an extremely noisy boiler factory. During that night, while he slept, he had learned to blot out the sounds of the factory and, by morning, he could hear the workers conversing in a normal conversational tone, something he had been unable to do the previous evening. The workers were surprised by this, as it had taken them much longer to master this ability, but Erickson said he knew how quickly the body could learn. He went on to tell the couple about seeing a television program the previous night about nomadic tribesmen in Iran who wore layers of clothing in the hot desert sun, but seemed very comfortable. As the session progressed, he told a variety of stories illustrating the ability people have to become habituated to any constant stimulus such that, after a while, they could learn to tune it out. "What people don't know is that they can lose that pain and they don't know that they can lose that ringing in the ears. . . . All of us grow up believing that when you have pain, you must pay attention to it. And believing when you have ringing of the ears that you must keep on hearing it" (Erickson & Rossi, 1979, p. 105).

A woman was referred for treatment of a "pregnancy phobia." It was discovered that the woman had previously been pregnant and had almost died several times during and after the pregnancy due to asthma and bronchitis. She was late for her expected menstrual bleeding that month and had become

quite anxious, with accompanying difficulty breathing. She
was told that the therapist did not think she had a phobia at
all, but a quite realistic fear, and he suggested that hypnosis be
used to see if it could help her "breathe easier." After inducing
a trance, the therapist reminded her that she had probably
experienced automatic muscle relaxation when in a hot bath.
He suggested complete body dissociation, as well as hand levi-
tation (both involving automatic muscle control). He recalled
a well-known commercial on television for a breathing medica-
tion that showed "blocked bronchial tubes" opening up and the
muscles around the bronchii relaxing. He told her that her
body had previously ended bronchitis and asthma attacks and
that her body therefore knew from that and other experiences
how to relax her bronchial muscles. She was seen several times
and experienced significant relief. She had also found out that
she was not pregnant. After she experienced such improvement, she and her husband decided to have the other child
they wanted. She came in irregularly throughout the course of
her pregnancy (for "booster shots") and experienced none of
the previous breathing difficulties.

METAPHOR THROUGH ACTION

Minuchin and Fishman describe how, in the therapy of a
family with a 14-year-old "anorectic" girl, Dr. Minuchin had
become increasingly of the opinion that family members were
using her to voice many of the things that they were unable or
unwilling to express to each other. Minuchin said to the girl,

" . . . Gina, you are caught because you are saying to your father the kinds of things that you think your mother wants to
tell your dad, so you amplify Mother's voice. You are saying to
your mommy the kind of things that you know your grandma
and your father say to your mother. So you are just the voice
of everybody in this family. You don't have your own voice.
You are the puppet of the ventriloquist. Have you ever seen a
ventriloquist? Sit on your mother's or your grandma's lap. Just
for a moment, sit on her lap. (Gina obeys.) Now tell your moth-

cr the way in which she should change, thinking like grandmother." (Minuchin & Fishman, 1981, pp. 132–138)

By asking the girl to sit on her grandmother's lap and to act
like a ventriloquist's dummy, Minuchin produced a brilliant
and powerful metaphor. By choosing the grandmother's lap,
he also made a powerful statement about the structure of the
family and the grandmother's role in its development. Although the book does not reveal the results of the intervention,
it is hard to imagine that such a dramatic experience could
have had no effect on the family.

Bodin and Ferber have described a home visit during the
therapy of a couple who were "singularly unexpressive, and
sexually inhibited." Seeing an organ in the corner of the room
and discovering that it was the wife who played it, albeit in a
somewhat solemn and unadventurous way, the therapist

> expressed surprise that a woman so concerned about doing
> things right would not have systematically explored the effects
> of each stop in turn and in various combinations. . . . She was
> asked to proceed with introducing these additional elements, in
> turn, but, in each instance, only after thoroughly enjoying the
> experience of letting her fingers massage the organ while savor-
> ing its tone. . . . (1972, pp. 297–298)

The authors went on to describe how a "faint smile as the
therapist spoke suggested that they (the couple) were listening
between the lines. . . . "

METAPHORICAL TASKS

de Shazer describes a family in which a mother and daughter continually bickered and the father attempted always to
be "fair" to both sides. The family was given the task of finding
a secluded spot to which it was to travel in silence. Mother
and daughter were then to have a water pistol fight. The father
was to carry a water supply and was to decide, as fairly as
possible, who won each round. The trip home was, again, to be
in silence. As the family became increasingly provoked into

laughter by the task, so the bickering somehow lessened until it was no longer a problem for the family (de Shazer, 1980). de Shazer cautions,

> families can accept such apparently absurd tasks when it is a metaphor for the real complaint pattern, and it is carefully designed so that it fits the family's unique manner of co-operating. Any sign from the family that they are rejecting the assignment means that the therapist has not found the family's way of co-operating, and therefore he should abort the planned intervention. . . . (de Shazer, 1980, p. 475)

"I ONCE KNEW A FAMILY WHO ..."

Referring to the experiences of another family, particularly where that family has made good progress with a similar problem, can both help people see that they are not alone in having difficulties and stimulate hope where other forms of encouragement and reassurance might have failed. Sometimes by revealing aspects of his or her own family experiences, a therapist can introduce new connections for a family, although care must be taken that the members not experience the therapist as being smug about himself or herself such that it highlights their own sense of failure. Sometimes a tale of another family's structure or its less successful experiences can stir a family into action to prove that the therapist would be wrong to assume that this family was going to be like that other family.

Finally, many of a therapist's actions will also carry metaphorical messages, whether they be deliberate or unconscious in intent. For example, at a very basic level, how he or she dresses, how the office is arranged and decorated, what photographs, certificates, or paintings deck the walls, how the therapist introduces him or herself and how the client or family is addressed, will all potentially carry messages that can influence how the contact with the therapist is experienced.

> Metaphor lets therapists address multiple dimensions of the system, thereby increasing the chances for connection with as-

pirations and difficulties that are outside of the client's conscious awareness. . . . Metaphor makes the learning process more graceful and interesting. It leaves people free to respond in ways that feel appropriate for them, including modifying or rejecting a suggested pattern. As it does with the other therapeutic processes, using metaphor in working with patterns allow therapists to adapt the therapeutic experience to fit their client's needs. (Combs & Freedman, 1990, p. 85)

12

PARADOXICAL INTERVENTIONS

"I think I'll go and meet her," said Alice, for, though the flowers were interesting enough, she felt that it would be far grander to have a talk with a real Queen.

"You can't possibly do that," said the Rose: "I should advise you to walk the other way."

This sounded nonsense to Alice, so she said nothing, but set off at once towards the Red Queen. To her surprise, she lost sight of her in a moment, and found herself walking in at the front-door again.

A little provoked, she drew back, and after looking everywhere for the Queen (whom she spied out as last, a long way off), she thought she would try the plan, this time, of walking in the opposite direction.

It succeeded beautifully. She had not been walking a minute before she found herself face to face with the Red Queen, and full in sight of the hill she had been so long aiming at.

— Through the Looking Glass, *Lewis Carroll*

Paradoxical interventions have fascinated many therapists, posed ethical dilemmas for some, and outraged others. This chapter will look briefly at the history of their use, will examine a number of ways that they have been conceptualized and will also present our current thinking on this intriguing way of intervening.

Many different approaches to therapy (e.g., existential, behavioral, psychoanalytic, interactional, and strategic) have used what were defined as paradoxical interventions, and each often had its own theory about when such interventions should be used and how they work. Watzlawick et al. defined a paradox as "a contradiction that follows correct deduction from consistent premises" (1967, p. 188). It is not our intention formally to explore the nature of paradox. However, at the pragmatic level, as far as therapy is concerned, it involves an explicit or implicit yet clear communication given to a client which is embedded within another explicit or implicit contradictory, frame-setting communication, such that a dilemma is produced. To comply with either one necessitates that the other be disobeyed. For example, Watzlawick et al. point out that the most common paradox in human communication is the demand from another (or oneself) for a particular emotional, attitudinal, or behavioral response that, however, will only be acceptable if it occurs spontaneously. For example, "I would like you to want to be more independent." The clear communication to "be spontaneous" is embedded within an equally clear frame-setting communication that demands obedience (p. 199). These two communications, given together, can only produce confusion or paralysis unless the subject of the demands can either point out the impossible nature of the situation (usually the more difficult action, the more dependent, insecure, or threatened a person feels in the relationship) or find some way to leave the field (sometimes extremely difficult, at other times, almost impossible).

Often, paradoxical techniques have been confused with, or seen as synonymous with, confrontation or challenge. A confrontation or challenge is given where a client is expected to respond directly by becoming motivated to prove either to himself or herself, to the therapist, or to some other person(s) that some difficulty can be faced or achieved, that the other person is wrong, or that they are not going to be ordered around. Either of these techniques involves a straightforward, though perhaps provocative, communication on the part of the therapist, not a paradoxical one.

Paradoxical techniques in therapy can be defined as those interventions in which the therapist, in a spirit of seeking to help, seems to promote the continuation or even the worsening of problems rather than their removal. A clear injunction to maintain or worsen a problem, or to slow down any improvement, is embedded in an equally clear frame-setting communication defining the context as one that is intended to help solve the problem. The approach has been reported as successful with symptoms such as phobias and obsessions (Frankl, 1970), tics (Yates, 1958), jealousy in couples (Teismann, 1979), migraine headaches (Gentry, 1973), temper tantrums (Breunlin et al., 1980), anorexia and encopresis (Palazzoli et al., 1974), and with the families of "schizophrenics" and "anorectics" (Palazzoli et al., 1975, 1978).

The use of paradoxical techniques can arguably be seen as dating back almost to the beginning of this century (although they probably go back much further). Mozdzierz, Maccitelli, and Lisiecki have shown how many of Alfred Adler's techniques were paradoxical in intention (Mozdzierz et al., 1976). In the 1920s, Dunlap evolved an approach called "negative practice" which involved the active practicing of symptoms such as nail-biting, stammering, and enuresis under prescribed conditions, the intention being that the habits would cease (Dunlap, 1928, 1930). In the 1930s, Frankl developed the technique of "paradoxical intention" in which phobic or obsessive patients were encouraged to try to bring on their symptoms rather than avoid them (Frankl, 1969, 1970). In the early 1950s, working with acutely psychotic patients, Rosen would encourage them to act out their most florid psychotic states and, later, when improvements occurred, prescribe a return to those states (1953).

In a bibliography of paradoxical methods, Weeks and L'Abate referred to the exponential growth in papers and chapters on paradox, a rate of growth that has since then showed little sign of slowing down (1978).

Over the last couple of decades, perhaps the most influential figures in this field have been Haley (1963, 1973), the staff of the Brief Therapy Center at the Mental Research Institute in Palo Alto, California (Fisch et al., 1982; Watzlawick, 1978; Watzlawick et al., 1967, 1974; Weakland et al., 1974), Palazzoli et al., of the Centro per lo Studio della Famiglia in Milan (Palazzoli et al., 1978), and Milton Erickson (Erickson & Rossi, 1979; Haley, 1967b, 1973; Rossi, 1980).

One of the most common and best known paradoxical techniques has been symptom prescription. The patient or family is advised or instructed to continue symptomatic or associated behaviors for the time being or to increase them, and this is usually explained as a way of ultimately solving the problem more quickly. Watzlawick et al. described this technique as posing the dilemma that the patient must do voluntarily what usually is claimed to be involuntary, "The symptomatic behavior is no longer spontaneous. . . . Something done 'because I can't help it' and the same behavior engaged in 'because my therapist told me to' could not be more different" (Watzlawick et al., 1967, p. 237). Symptomatic behavior could also be "prescribed" with the explanation that it was in order to avoid the possibility, were the original problem to disappear, of a different or worse problem emerging, either in the patient or in his or her intimates.

Michael Rohrbaugh and his colleagues distinguished between *compliance-based* prescriptions, where a continuation or increase in symptomatic behaviors is requested, with a reasonable expectation that the patient will attempt to cooperate with the therapist, and *defiance-based* prescriptions, where the expectation is that the patient will defy the therapist's requests, either overtly or covertly (Rohrbaugh et al., 1977, 1981). The former were seen as being effective because the patient attempts to comply and finds it impossible to do so or experiences compliance as an aversive ordeal. The latter can be effective because the patient resists or rebels against the prescription and therefore reduces or renounces symptomatic behaviors. Brehm's theory of psychological reactance (1966) was used to help determine which class of prescription to use. Two parameters were seen as important: first, the extent to which a patient tended to be reactant or oppositional to therapy, and second, the extent to which the patient saw the symptoms as being largely within or outside of his or her control. Rohrbaugh et al. proposed that, where opposition is low and symptoms are seen by the patient as outside of control, then compliance-based prescriptions are indicated. Where opposition is high and symptoms are seen by the patient as potentially controllable, then defiance-based prescriptions are indicated. Where opposition is low and symptoms are seen as controllable, paradoxical approaches are seen as unnecessary. High opposition with symptoms seen as uncontrollable represents, they suggested, the most difficult combination to deal with unless a degree of compliance can somehow be elicited (Rohrbaugh et al., 1977, 1981).

Tennen classified paradoxes under three headings: *prescribing, restraining,* and *positioning* (1977). When restraining, the therapist discourages the patient from changing or denies the possibility that change can occur. Tennen explained, "for example, he may tell the patient to 'go slow,' or emphasize the dangers of improvement. In selected cases, he may even suggest that the situation is hopeless." This latter approach would usually only be indicated with highly oppositional patients. Positioning was described as attempting to "shift a problematic 'position'—usually an assertion that the patient is making about himself or his problem—by accepting or exaggerating that position." For example, Watzlawick et al. tell of a young college student, recently discharged from a mental institution following a psychotic episode, whose utopian ambitions were to influence the Western world through his music.

> [He] also wanted to study agriculture in order to utilize Chinese agricultural methods to feed the starving masses of the world. When the therapist agreed with these goals in principle but found them not sufficiently big, the patient countered this by beginning to talk about a far less ambitious plan, namely to get involved in a halfway house. . . . By consistently using this technique, the therapist was able to bring the dialogue down to more and more practical levels. (Watzlawick et al., 1974, pp. 153–154)

Cade and Southgate described the successful treatment of an obese, depressed, and "inadequate" single mother. The therapist, in a spirit of benevolent concern, would continually highlight the lists of negative or critical statements the woman continually made about herself, either by validating her reasons for despair, by suggesting that things were perhaps worse than the woman was admitting, and by cautioning against trying too much, too quickly (Cade & Southgate, 1979). (Interestingly, in a subsequent follow-up visit, the woman identified the therapist's "honesty" as the most important and helpful facet of the therapy.)

Fisher, Anderson, and Jones distinguished three classes of paradoxical strategy:

a. *Redefinition.* This they defined as an attempt to alter the meaning or the interpretation placed on symptoms and seen as most appropriate with families possessing some capacity for reflection and insight. For example, a young, single mother complained that her son, whenever she brought a man friend home, would behave atrociously, swearing, sometimes behaving aggressively towards the man and refusing to leave them alone together. At the end of the first session the boy was defined by the therapist as extremely sensitive and aware of his mother's underlying fear of becoming emotionally involved again and being hurt, in the way that his father had hurt her. His "bad" behaviors were an attempt to protect her from men by driving them away. Only a man who "really" loved her would stand by her in the face of such provocation. At the next session the mother reported vast improvements in her son's behavior.

b. *Escalation.* This is an attempt to create a crisis or to increase the frequency of symptomatic behavior. They described a family in which a husband's hypochondria was seen as apparently maintaining a rather enmeshed family pattern. The man was instructed to log every thought and physical problem, record blood pressure and heart rate at 15-minute intervals, and report to his doctor twice daily. The rest of the family was given detailed instructions of how they were to help. The husband soon became "sick" of the routine and began to take part in family activities again. Escalation was described as most applicable in rigid families where resistance is high.

c. *Redirection.* This is changing an aspect of a symptom, for example, prescribing particular circumstances for symptomatic behavior. A "shop-phobic" woman was taken on a shopping expedition and given careful instructions about when she should start experiencing feelings of nausea and where exactly to faint in order to avoid the crowds. After half an hour she had experienced no panic and went on to spend some time on her own looking for a gift for her daughter. A year later there had been no recurrence of the symptoms. This strategy was described as more appropriate with cooperative patients or families where resistance is low. (Fisher et al., 1981)

The early work of Palazzoli et al. with families of "anorexics" or "schizophrenics" had an enormous impact on the field of family therapy (Palazzoli, 1974; Palazzoli et al., 1975, 1978, 1980a). They developed a systemic approach using the resources of a team and concerned primarily with the way that symptoms reflect the "rules" of a family system (or "the family game"). They highlighted the importance of placing a positive connotation on such family "rules" and on the behavior of all family members, including that of the symptomatic member, however bizarre, and even, where appropriate, on those family members who were apparent victimizers. For all attitudes and behaviors, a positive connotation proposed motives that had the unity and stability of the family group at heart. It implied approval of the motives underlying those behaviors, thus placing all family members together so that "they are complementary in relation to the system, without in any way connoting them moralistically, thus avoiding any drawing of a dividing line between members of the group" (Palazzoli et al., 1978, p. 61). Only by defining positively each member's part in the "family game" could the therapist logically proceed to prescribe that "game" in order, paradoxically, to facilitate change. Interventions were thus based on allying totally with what was described as the "homeostatic" tendencies of the family. An explicit or implicit prescription was given that no change should occur *for the time being*. It can be seen that reframing played an important part in these interventions, with each family member's role and behaviors being given a new meaning (framed as being for the benefit of the family as a whole). Considerable attention was also paid to the role of other professionals, previously or currently involved, in the development and maintenance of a problem (Palazzoli et al., 1980b).

Papp also described paradoxical techniques utilizing the potentials for triangulation inherent in a team approach, with the observers acting as a "Greek chorus," selectively commenting on the therapy process and making recommendations, often of a prescriptive or restraining nature (Papp, 1980). Breunlin and Cade described the use of observer messages for intervening in family systems (1981), while Cornwell and Pearson commented on the degree of cooperation and coordination needed when devising such messages (1981). Cade elaborated the use of contrived team conflicts reflecting nodal struggles within families with a prescription that no change be attempted until the team has unraveled its dilemma, as a way of resolving what were seen as therapeutic deadlocks (Cade, 1980a). The formulation of such teams and the advantages and problems of working in this way were explored by members of the Family Institute team in Cardiff, Wales (Cade et al., 1986; Speed et al., 1982).

There has been no unified theoretical framework for describing and understanding paradoxical psychotherapy. Watzlawick et al., using Whitehead and Russell's Theory of Logical Types (Whitehead & Russell, 1910–13), proposed two levels of change, *first order* and *second order*, the former described changes that do not involve the reorganization of the whole system, the latter referred to changes in the system itself and in its "rules" (Watzlawick et al., 1974). Paradoxical techniques were seen as moving outside of the class of first-order "attempted solutions," leading to the possibilities of second-order change. Weeks and L'Abate proposed a dialectical approach to understanding the nature of paradoxical therapy utilizing a model of pathology based on Karpman's drama triangle (Weeks, 1977; Weeks & L'Abate, 1982). Family members were described as becoming bound by the three roles of "persecutor," "rescuer," and "victim." Paradoxical techniques were seen as exposing the deception behind the appearance of powerlessness in the victim role and power in the roles of persecutor and rescuer through the prescription of such roles. Other writers have accentuated the importance of the "unexpected" positions taken by the therapist in disrupting patterns of belief and action (Cade, 1991; Palazzoli, 1981). As Dell observed, "paradoxical therapy, much like Pirandello's play, remains a set of techniques in search of a theory" (Dell, 1981, p. 41).

A number of writers have attempted to elaborate the contraindications against using paradoxical techniques. Fisher, Anderson, and Jones listed four categories: (a) chaotic families with loose and variable structures; (b) child-like families in which all members, including adults, are very immature and seeking parenting from the therapist; (c) impulsive families with overly hostile members; and (d) families that accept responsibilities and offer minimal opposition (Fisher et al., 1981). Weeks and L'Abate include clients who are not committed or involved actively in therapy, sociopaths, the paranoid who may sense the "deceit," and where there is the potential for destructive behavior (e.g., homicidal or suicidal tendencies) (1982). Rohrbaugh et al. suggested that contraindications exist in situations of grief reaction and acute loss of status (1977).

The use of paradoxical techniques has, perhaps understandably, raised for many the issue of professional ethics. The approach was seen by some as overtly "manipulative," "controlling," and even "dishonest," and perhaps dangerous in that people are encouraged to escalate symptomatic behavior. These criticisms have been addressed by several writers. Watzlawick et al. (1974) and Haley pointed out how all therapy and communication inevitably involves a greater or lesser degree of manipulation. As manipulation is thus unavoidable, they suggest that the therapist is ethically bound to use this inevitability to the patient's or family's best advantage. Haley comments that "the pretense that sitting with a deadpan expression and responding in monosyllables would not influence a patient's life decisions had been recognized as only a pretense" (Haley, 1976, p. 200). From this perspective, the question thus becomes not whether or not to "manipulate," but how much and in what way will be best for any particular case. One argument to counter this position has been to differentiate between the unconscious influence and counter-influence inevitable in all relationships, and the deliberate use of manipulation in which the therapist sets out to effect outcomes or to address agendas that lie outside of the awareness of the client. It is certainly our belief that brief therapists have, at times, been somewhat cavalier in their use of paradoxical interventions.

Weeks and L'Abate have referred to the ethical responsibility not to use paradoxical techniques either as a gimmick or out of frustration when therapy seems stuck or patients seem uncooperative (1982). They underlined the importance of the therapist making responsible decisions based not only on intuition but also on the basis of careful analytic judgment. They observed that, at the time of writing, they knew of no evidence that paradoxical techniques had caused a deterioration in any patient; the worst that happened was that no change occurs. They pointed out, in answer to criticisms about "control," that patients often attributed changes to their own efforts, thus potentially seeing themselves in more positive ways, a phenomenon for which evidence was found by Frude and Dowling (1980). However, Weeks and L'Abate cautioned that, "despite the fact that hundreds of case studies have been reported demonstrating the unusual effectiveness of this approach, there has been very little empirical work of any kind" (1982, p. 219).

PARADOX RECONSIDERED: EMPATHY, NOT TRICKERY

It is no longer our view that paradoxical interventions operate as power tactics, tricks, or through the production of therapeutic double-binds with all loopholes sealed off. All of us are likely to experience ambivalence when faced with any significant challenge to, or a need to change, established patterns of thinking or of acting. This will be particularly so when those patterns relate to the more significant dimensions (to us) through which we draw distinctions and make sense of ourselves and our experiences.

Ambivalence can be seen as the concurrent existence of opposing arguments and constructs which can be brought to bear when contemplating significant change and which will produce varied affective responses. Some of these can be articulated clearly while others may exist more unconsciously or at a more instinctual level. When a therapist becomes too clearly identified with the arguments in favor of change, whether this position be explicitly or implicitly communicated, it is as though he or she colonizes those arguments, leaving available to the client or family members only the counter-arguments (or the "yes, buts") to that change together with the accompanying affect produced by those counter-arguments.

.Conversely, when a therapist identifies with and validates the arguments in favor of caution or against change from a position of having joined effectively with family members, by a similar process, family members are then left, as it were, with ownership of the counter-arguments (or the "yes, buts") to those cautions (i.e., in favor of the change). As we have pointed out earlier, research on persuasion has shown that we are much more likely to be persuaded by self-generated arguments and counter-arguments than by the arguments of others.

It is our view that what have previously been termed paradoxical strategies have the effect of empowering clients through the process of acknowledging their perfectly valid cautious, more fearful concerns about change and leaving them then to operate out of their own arguments as to why change should be attempted. With their conscious or less conscious arguments in favor of change colonized, they tend to respond with explicit or implicit "yes, buts" reflecting their arguments against. However, with their arguments *against* validated and colonized, they tend to respond with explicit or implicit "yes, buts" reflecting their arguments in favor of change.

We use the term "colonization" deliberately in that, no matter how benevolent the colonizer, the process of colonization is one of a lessening of self-determination and control over choices on the part of the colonized.

When people enter therapy, they at times have a complaint that involves some experience or behavior that they would like to have occur less frequently or not at all, and that they experience as beyond their control; or, alternatively, some experience or result that they would like to achieve or have happen more frequently but that they perceive themselves as unable to attain.

When the therapist finds that the more the client tries to eliminate the unwanted, the more it occurs, or the more the client tries to attain a desired result, the more elusive it seems to become, then some kind of paradoxical intervention might be called for. However, the point we would make here is that it is not appropriate to go about "paradoxing" clients (or, as we have once heard it called, "zapping them with a paradox") because it seem a good technique that has worked at times. We now find that a cooperative and respectful "paradoxical intention," usually quite openly and sometimes humorously suggested — somewhat in the style of Victor Frankl — will often help break the deadlock (Frankl, 1969, 1970).

We now find ourselves rarely, if ever, using covert and deceptive interventions. However, we here intend no sanctimonious, "holier-than-thou" comments on erstwhile paradoxical therapists. After all, we have been numbered among their ranks. It is just that our ideas about therapy have evolved over time. Along with the majority of our colleagues, we no longer see therapy in the same adversarial way that we used to. However, during those heady days during which we did see therapy in those terms, brief therapists gained considerable knowledge about, and a respect for, people's abilities to change and also about the process of therapy, knowledge upon which the current generation of therapists is now able to build.

13

OVERRESPONSIBILITY AND UNDERRESPONSIBILITY: OPPOSITE SIDES OF THE COIN

Gratitude is hatred in a mask.

— Frederick Nietzsche

The love least likely to let anyone down continues to be a bargain struck between self-interest and self interest. . . .

— Julian Fane (1988)

A person who wants to repay a gift too quickly with a gift in return is an unwilling debtor and an ungrateful person.

— Indian proverb

A child of any age may suddenly need to be responsible, perhaps because of the death of a parent or because of the break-up of a family. Such a child must be prematurely old and must lose spontaneity and play and carefree creative impulse.

— D. Winnicott

At a workshop some years ago, I was showing a videotape of a family with a 17-year-old girl who was bulimic and a 14-

This chapter is a paper by Brian Cade, printed in its entirety, with minor revisions, that originally appeared in *The Journal of Family Therapy*, Spring 1989, pp. 103–121. It is reprinted with the kind permission of the Editors of the journal.

year-old girl who was beginning seriously to act out. The interview involved three generations of the family including the girls' twice-divorced mother, hard-working and bitter, and her mother, who seemed to be intrusively "helpful" and overinvolved with the family. I observed to the group that, being the child of a parent, or parents, who unselfishly sacrificed themselves and their own needs on your behalf, who gave their all, yet seemed unwilling or unable to take anything in return, in spite of their own considerable needs, could lead to the development in the child of increasing feelings of obligation, guilt, unworthiness, and a feeling that she did not deserve nor could ever repay such a sacrifice. That the parent would not ask to be repaid seemed only to compound the problem. I went on to suggest that such children might experience considerable difficulties in leaving home, and that there were four, basically interchangeable, pathologies that might be likely to develop under the burden of such feelings, three of which were being manifested in the family on the tape. I presented them to the workshop in the following order of increasing seriousness:

1. They could seek to justify their existences and to "repay their debt" by becoming the same in their interactions with others, sacrificing themselves and taking nothing in return, particularly for their own children, such that the feelings of obligation and unworthiness inadvertently become transmitted to the next generation. Such people often fail in outside relationships, remain close to their parents' home, and sometimes remain living within it.
2. They could attempt to reject the burden by acting out, by rejecting the "obligations." In such attempts, extremes of behavior or attitudes unacceptable to the family and to society might often be used in order to reach the necessary "escape velocity." However, such people will often remain isolated, resentful, guilty, and desperate for acceptance, frequently ending up in "persecutor/rescuer" relationships, or failing in their lives and returning home.
3. They could withdraw from the field through developing a psychiatric condition.

4. They could become very responsible members of the various helping professions and seek to justify their lives by helping others.

Although this latter was introduced almost as a lighthearted, throw-away line, I was surprised by the reaction of many of the participants in the workshop. Some became very upset, and many approached me later to say how accurately I had described many aspects of their own family backgrounds and their past and current dilemmas. This paper is in response to the many professionals who, then and subsequently, have asked me whether I had written anything about this phenomenon.

THREE LEVELS OF RESPONSIBILITY

According to Dorothy Sayer's fictional character Lord Peter Wimsey, "Life is just one damn thing after another." It is my belief that family members are best able to deal with this fact of life when three levels of responsibility are *equally addressed at all times* (except, of course, at times of crisis, or for brief periods owing to specific circumstances):

1. an appropriate level of responsibility is taken as a parent for the development and well-being of children, encouraging the development of autonomy; or, as a grown-up child, for the well-being of sick or aging relatives;
2. responsibility is taken as a spouse for the continued development of the marriage including the showing of an appropriate level of concern for, and consideration of, your partner's needs and interests; and
3. responsibility is taken for seeing to your own needs and for your own continued development as a separate individual.

Constant overfunctioning in any one of these areas, with the consequent neglect of the other areas, will lead to less and less flexibility and a greater probability that problems will develop around one or more of life's seemingly endless supply of difficulties. As the husband of a middle-aged couple recently said to me, after describing how they had been struggling for years bringing up their children, particularly their extremely demanding, youngest son, as well as looking after the husband's aging and also very demanding mother:

> We realize now that we have become just a limited series of formal roles rather than a man and a woman with needs of our own who happen also to be mother, father, spouse, offspring, etc., and now nothing we've done seems to have been right or, in the long term, to have helped. Now we're both totally exhausted. We feel that we have failed our son, I feel I have failed my parents, and we both feel we have failed each other.

Ivan Boszormenyi-Nagy (Boszormenyi-Nagy & Krasner, 1986; Boszormenyi-Nagy & Spark, 1984) has developed an approach to therapy based on looking at intergenerational, transactional patterns in terms of ledgers of accountability and entitlement, justice and fairness, loyalty and trust, and at the consequences of exploitative relationships on others, particularly on children. Perhaps because of the complexity of his writing style, his tendency towards dogmatism and moralization, and perhaps also because of his dismissive attacks on the essentially here-and-now focus of the structural, strategic, systemic, and behavioral approaches, his work has had a less significant impact on the field of family therapy than it otherwise might have done. I consider this a loss in that his contribution to the understanding of global intergenerational themes and patterns has been profound, even though the specific repetitive patterns of thought and behavior through which such patterns are developed, transmitted, and maintained are not dealt with in any detail in his works.

In considering the consequences of overfunctioning, Boszormenyi-Nagy and Spark propose that,

> Inherent in all close and meaningful relationships are the fundamental elements of giving and receiving, of being treated fairly or unjustly, of taking without repaying, or receiving with no possibility of giving back. Martyrdom or over-giving and permissiveness, scapegoating, and parentification are illustrations

of nonbalancing or nonmutual reciprocity within relationships. Such relationships stimulate feelings of guilt and perpetual indebtedness; they also produce feelings of despair, as if one could never settle family accounts—either through emotional interest and concern or by concrete actions.

Since we assume as a basic postulate that every child receives from his parents and implicitly owes them repayment, a parental unwillingness to receive is considered as detrimental as a parental inability to give. (1984, p. 353)

FORMATIVE EXPERIENCES

A tendency to take on the role of the overresponsible (or, conversely, the irresponsible) member in any relationship or set of relationships can have its genesis in a variety of different formative environments, of which the following have cropped up most regularly in my practice:

1. a chaotic and conflictual, unhappy and rejecting environment in which an inappropriate and often excessive degree of responsibility for controling the chaos and caring for others is delegated by the parents or other adults to a child or adolescent. Though this is explicitly or implicitly demanded of them, they are rarely praised, their efforts are usually taken for granted and often criticized or ridiculed. They invariably will suffer feelings of unworthiness and, however hard they have tried, see their family's continued problems as evidence of their failure.
2. a chaotic, conflictual, rejecting environment in which a child or adolescent takes on to their *own* shoulders an inappropriate and excessive degree of responsibility for trying to control the chaos and to care for other members, children or adults. As with the previous group, they are rarely thanked; they are often taken for granted, usually resented and tend to suffer feelings of failure, unworthiness, and blame.
3. a chaotic environment or an overcontrolled, rigid, unhappy environment in which a child or adolescent is parentified and pulled constantly into a collusion with an adult and delegated the responsibility for that adult's well-being.
4. an environment, chaotic or otherwise, in which a child or ado-

lescent feels themselves to have been the undeserving recipient of, and thus the cause of, an adult's constant self-sacrifice, particularly where the adult appears to have been either unable or unwilling to receive anything back in return.
5. the experience of being unwanted, rejected, scapegoated, or abused, leading to feelings of *being* bad ("otherwise it wouldn't have happened to me") and thus leading either to constant attempts to achieve acceptance by trying to be good, or to an acceptance of the "bad" role.

Prevailing cultural myths about the role relationships and responsibility in relationships will of course have a significant effect. Women in most cultures are usually expected to take the responsibility for nurturing and for the emotional climate in the family. Many myths about the inherent attitudinal and behavioral differences between the sexes still prevail, have become institutionalized, and are perpetuated through custom and self-fulfilling prophecies. For example, the myths that women are more emotional, intuitive, patient, and loving than men, that men are braver and stronger, more rational, more aggressive and sexual, better at abstract thinking, more skillful with their hands, etc., are still enshrined in tradition and often encouraged as virtues. I have also found that religious teachings that highlight sinfulness and guilt, humility and obedience, obligation and self-denial, and the injunction that it is more blessed to give than to receive, are frequently a current or past and formative feature of families where one or more members are constantly overfunctioning in a self-sacrificial way. Although this paper is concerned primarily with those situations where over/underfunctioning has become a marked feature, the themes will, to a greater or lesser extent, affect all families as well as other groups.

THE RESPONSIBILITY–IRRESPONSIBILITY CONTINUUM

The predominantly negative self-constructs and constructs about relationships (Kelly, 1955) that arise out of the experiences of environments such as those elaborated above can then lead to the development of a range of "attempted solutions" to the dilemmas posed that will tend to cluster at either end of the following continuum:

Overresponsible ─────────────────── Underresponsible

varied attempts to control the relationships in their environment by assuming complete responsibility and by trying to impose their definition of how things ought to be	varied attempts to avoid being controlled by those in their environment by acting out, rebelling, or through "underadequate" behaviors

Being opposites in a dialectic *within* their personal construct systems, either extreme is usually equally possible, and people can also alternate between either end, although once patterns have become established in any relationship or set of relationships, the self-fulfilling power of the attributions and expectations of all involved usually leads to a tendency for an individual to settle at one end or other of the continuum.

For example, in a paper looking at the adolescent experiences of 50 adult female suicide attempters, Stephens found that there was much in common in the family backgrounds of the women in the study group, which had left them with a legacy of depression, guilt, anger, and feelings of worthlessness (1987). However, she was surprised to find two seemingly opposite patterns of adaptation, one which she labeled "Humble Pie," the other "Cheap Thrills."

"Humble Pie"	**"Cheap Thrills"**
tended towards:	tended towards:
– over-conformity; trying hard to please	– defiant rebellion; deliberate intentions to be a "bad girl"; anger at the family environment that exploited them
– trying to be "perfect"; justifying themselves through over-achievement	

- guilty responsibility; a sense of failure
- submersion in the problems of their families, which become *their* failures
- attempting to control the variables in their lives via compulsive, even paranoid, adherence to strict rules and standards (sometimes of others, but often of their own)
- submergence of their own needs and rights
- self-sacrifice, always putting others first
- martyrdom

- truancy; poor school performances
- involvement with drug taking, alcohol and promiscuous sex
- reactions against control by others, sometimes extreme
- growing up feeling hated and hateful
- frequent violent physical confrontations both with family members and with boyfriends; multiple shallow relationships outside the family

The "Humble Pie" group tended to come from more middle-class families where anger and acting-out were probably less acceptable, and thus feelings of resentment were more likely to be internalized and experienced as proof of their own badness. The "Cheap Thrills" group tended to come from more working-class families where aggression would probably be more accepted and thus more easily externalized. The former group apparently were more likely to make multiple attempts on their lives and to employ more violent means. Stephens goes on to conclude that, "The clinical implications of the Humble Pie pattern are sobering, in that they suggest that there is a population greatly at risk that may not have been identified by either researchers or suicide prevention workers. The Cheap Thrills adolescents draw attention to themselves and their problems, whereas the Humble Pie adolescents may remain invisible" (p. 117).

Neither extreme seems to solve the dilemmas posed by their experiences. As Boszormenyi-Nagy and Spark observe, "the exploited child often turns into a symbiotically possessive parent" (1984, p. 28). "Acts of rebellion or escape through separation can never in themselves resolve the child's predicament. These measures just sink him deeper into guilt-burdened obligations. Many children become angrily ambivalent captives of never-repayable obligations" (p. 353). Or, as Stephens comments, "Both patterns of adaptation — Cheap Thrills and Humble Pie — proved in the long run to be dysfunctional for these women. . . . Neither was able to deflect the deepening sense of worthlessness and hopelessness that undermined these individuals' feelings about themselves and their world" (1987, p. 117).

Representatives of either end of the continuum will tend to choose as partners people struggling with similar issues. The patterns that then develop are likely to fall into one of the following three groups:

1. Both can evolve an overresponsible coalition in order to deal with their children (who will be likely to develop problems, particularly in relation to trust and responsibility), with other relatives, or with the outside world (including people from group 2), through becoming professional helpers, pressure group activists, etc. They will form a hidden group, as with the Humble Pie group described above, and can often appear to be model citizens.

2. Both can evolve an irresponsible, chaotic coalition, depending on, yet resenting and resisting, the efforts of a parentified child to help, the efforts of other relatives, or of the outside world in the shape of professional helpers, neighbors, the police, etc. (and people from group 1).

3. They can develop a complementary style of relationship in which one becomes responsible/adequate in inverse proportion to the other's irresponsibility/inadequacy (and *vice versa*). As Boszormenyi-Nagy and Spark observe, "overadequate family members can depend on the failure of under-adequate members" (1984, p. 24). I would also add that under-adequate family members can depend on the failure of over-adequate members.

Sharon was the youngest of four children. At 21 years of age, she had already been married twice, the second time to a violent young man with a criminal record who had badly beaten her and her two young children, now in the care of the local authorities. At the time, Sharon had been on drugs, fought constantly with her family, and was adjudged to be untrustworthy and not to have given the children adequate protection. According to her parents, she had been a major problem for them since the age of 14.

Sharon's mother described herself as the product of a very difficult childhood in which she was forced, by her father's desertion of her "inadequate" mother, prematurely to take considerable levels of responsibility, and learned to judge herself harshly. She grew up with a determination that her own children would always come first and never experience the harshness and loneliness of her upbringing. She had always put her own needs last, having learned to expect nothing for herself. She was wary of trusting men. She measured herself against self-imposed high standards of responsibility for, and the importance of giving to, others. Always available to answer the needs and demands of her family, she felt guilty whenever she perceived herself as falling short of her own impossible standards. And yet she had failed: With a broken marriage behind her, her oldest daughter and her child was now back at home (and much of the responsibility for the grandson was being left to her); her only son was substantially handicapped by a congenital eye condition; her third child was currently struggling unhappily in a troubled marriage; and now the youngest, Sharon, was in serious trouble with the authorities. Nevertheless, she saw it as her duty to protect Sharon from the opinion of the authorities and from the disappointed anger (she had been his favorite) of her husband.

Sharon's father was the "accidently conceived, youngest child of a broken home" who had spent much of his childhood in residential care. His mother had "tried her hardest but she just couldn't cope on her own with so many of us to look after. I can't blame her. She really was a saint." A hard-working, private man, cautious and guarded in relationships, he was sad that his affection for his children had been, as he saw it, swamped over the years by his wife's constant involvement with them. He admitted to a peripheral position in the family, admitted he was not particularly good at expressing his feelings, and spoke reluctantly but movingly of the difficulty of persuading his wife ever to take anything for herself. Any money he ever gave to her would be spent on the children. If he bought her a dress, she would complain that he shouldn't have done it and, often, would take it back to the shop to exchange it for something for the children or grandchildren. His role in the family was primarily as material provider, a job he discharged conscientiously. However, it seemed that he was, in many ways, treated like one of the children by his wife, sometimes tolerantly and indulgently, sometimes with exasperation. His undemonstrative, emotional "incompetence" and unavailability, both as a husband and as a father, and his focus mainly on things outside of the family, seemed, in turn, to have fed into her feelings of being "on her own," unsupported and unappreciated, confirming her feelings of unworthiness and her belief that her family's well-being was totally her responsibility. He admitted he was hurt and disappointed by what had happened but would not hear of Sharon's returning home again until she had proven that she could be trusted.

When I saw her, Sharon admitted that she did not like herself. She declared that she now had no more interest in men or in sex. She appeared to have become caught up in the dilemma highlighted by Groucho Marx's famous quip, "I would never be a member of a club that would have me as a member." Having little respect for herself, she would have difficulty in trusting anyone who would consider her as a potential partner. However, she had begun to settle down and was hoping eventually to get her children back. She was desperately unhappy at her father's rejection of her, though she blamed herself totally for this, and hoped eventually to be able to prove to him that she had changed her ways. She idealized both parents and aspired to be just like her mother, although she was unable to see herself "ever as being as good." Already she was seeing motherhood as continually considering the needs of her children first. Like her mother, she was beginning to see herself primarily in terms of what she did for, or gave to others, with a high premium being placed on tangible/material rather than emotional criteria for judging the quality of her mothering. Already she was setting herself unattainable standards in order to "make it up to the children for the dreadful things that I let happen to them," while, at the same time, anticipating her almost certain failure to achieve them.

Sharon's mother had been precipitated early into responsibility, yet unthanked and abused for her efforts; her father had been a "rejected" child, unable to be angry because his mother was "a saint" who had tried her best. He was brought up in residential homes where unassertive compliance rather than individuality was rewarded. The two of them married and formed a complementary relationship in which she was the overresponsible, he the "inadequate," underfunctioning, family member. Their children had been the recipients of unselfish devotion from a self-sacrificing mother, a hardworking but peripheral father. They were now all beginning to fail in their relationships outside of the family. The oldest daughter was back at home depending heavily on her mother, neglecting her responsibilities to her own child. Sharon had attempted to reject the "obligations" and had briefly formed a chaotic coalition with her violent second husband, but now was trying to return home, intending to emulate her mother and regain her father's love by denying her own rights to separateness and continuing the family tradition, sacrificing herself for her children.

This family was referred to me with the stated goals (stated at a case conference where the outlook was extremely skeptical that anything could be achieved) that I should try to help Sharon with her massive self-esteem problems and encourage her gradually to become more responsible. These goals were sufficiently achieved so that her children were soon returned to her and she moved into a small apartment with them. This goal was reached, however, not by working with Sharon, except quite briefly to predict and discuss with her probable early "re-entry problems," nor by seeing the whole family, but mainly by seeing Sharon's mother to persuade her to become more selfish and less helpful, to be more neglectful of her children and grandchildren. This was initially achieved by defining her actions as the difficult but necessary sacrifice of an obviously devoted mother/grandmother in order to help her daughter become a more effective and appropriately independent mother so that she could be reunited with her young children. However, interestingly, she soon began to pursue the path of increased "selfishness," not out of a sense of duty, but because she was beginning to enjoy herself, to realize that she had rights, and because she and her husband were beginning to enjoy more time together. She bought herself her first pretty and rather expensive dress, instead of a sensible one suitable for doing the housework and wearing to the supermarket. She began to say "no" to the demands of her children, initially a strange experience for her. As though released from their "obligations" by their mother's newfound freedom and their parents' improved relationship, Sharon and her siblings began to take much more responsibility for themselves.

Central to the success of this therapy seemed to be first, the careful mapping out of the intergenerational pattern with the mother and with the father such that they were both able to identify the effects on themselves of the sense of "obligation" and feelings of unworthiness they had inherited from their backgrounds (the pattern, and the personal constructs that had arisen as a result of it, rather than the individuals in it, was defined as responsible); and second, the targeting of specific behaviors that tended to maintain the pattern and the seeking out of ways of blocking or replacing them. For example, it was suggested to the mother that she should be prepared to babysit only once a week rather than being permanently available, to cook one evening meal at a pre-stated time rather than lecturing to and/or cooking for those who come in late, announcing unprovocatively that unfortunately they had missed dinner but they could rustle up something from the fridge if they were hungry and also, while they were out there, she would love a cup of tea.

PERSONAL CONSTRUCT SYSTEMS

Whatever the intergenerational experiences have been, it is the repetition of specific interactions arising out of the limitations of current construct systems that maintains and perpetuates the pattern. Some examples of the more common limiting personal construct systems are as follows:

"If I remain patient, loving and loyal regardless of how badly I am treated by him/her/them, then eventually . . . "
"What I achieve is my duty, the very least I can do. I have no *right* to feel good about it."
"I will do anything to make sure my children do not suffer in the way that I/we did."
"I am a failure and am worthless unless I can achieve . . . "
"I am only defined by what I do for others, but what I do will always fall short of what I ought to do."
"Whatever I do is going to be wrong or not good enough, anyway, therefore I might as well . . . "
"I can never repay them for what they did for me, neither did I deserve it. I ought to feel more grateful."
"For what they did to me/us, I hold my parents in low regard, even contempt. I am furious that I could never trust them. However, I expect and demand total and spontaneous loyalty from you (although I suspect, eventually, that you will betray the trust I am investing in you)."
"Nobody can be trusted so, if I do not take the ultimate responsibility, then . . . "
"Everyone else's happiness is what makes me happy" or "Everyone else's happiness must come before mine however much it costs me emotionally or physically."

Such constructs become embedded within people's life scripts. As Sartre said, "A man is always a teller of tales, he lives surrounded by his stories and the stories of others, he sees everything that happens to him through them; and he tries to live his life as if he were recounting it" (1965). When reviewing with people the intergenerational influences that can be seen as underpinning their constructs, I am not seeking to give them an insight into something that *is*, but to take the position "it is as if . . . ," which is where my work differs from the psychoanalytically based approach of Boszormenyi-Nagy. George Wald, an American scientist has proposed that, "We are the products of editing, rather than authorship." I see the process of therapy as more akin to reediting; going through a person's story and helping them rewrite parts of it. I take a similar position to Sartre, who declared, "I am not fond of the word psychological. There is no such thing as psychological. Let us say that one can improve the biography of the person" (Quoted unreferenced in Laing, 1965, p. 120).

"YOU DON'T KEEP A DOG AND BARK YOURSELF"

Keith and Whitaker have observed: "Parents can fail operationally by being too much of anything:

- too disciplining
- too ambivalent
- too decisive
- too protective
- too rejecting
- too loving

- too rigid
- too understanding
- too encouraging
- too crazy
- too impatient
- too lenient (1985, p. 10)

It appears that, whenever anyone in a relationship begins, from whatever motivation, to do too much of something, often the other member or members, if they are not moved directly to compete, will tend to start doing less of that something and/ or more of an opposite something. For example, a common sequence will often evolve where one parent views the other as too strict and therefore compensates by becoming more lenient with their children. Seeing this will usually lead to the first parent reacting by becoming more concerned about discipline. This increase in strictness will lead to an increase in leniency in the other, and so on, until the parents become totally polarized and it becomes as if one "owns" all of the strictness and the other all of the softness. Though there is no finite quantity of either strictness or leniency in the relationship, nor is the pattern a zero-sum game* (Von Neuman & Morgenstern, 1944),

A zero-sum game is one in which, whenever one player gains, the other player loses by an equal amount. What is gained and what is lost, when added together, always totals zero.

yet it is as if this is the case. Another common pattern occurs where one partner attempts constantly to persuade or push the other to become more expressive of their feelings. Very quickly they can polarize around the issue. The way they polarize seems to say little about their true potentials.

A couple, at the point of breaking up, came to therapy for "one last attempt to sort things out." She was sensitive, emotionally open, and expressive; he was distant, rational, and emotionally cool. She was constantly trying to get him to "open up." He saw her as totally irrational and never satisfied, whatever he did. They finally decided to separate, and I helped them do this with the maximum of self-respect and dignity. Several months later, another woman referred herself. She described herself as sensitive, needy, emotionally open, and expressive. She described her husband as cold, unresponsive, and totally unemotional. Asked why she had sought help now, she told me she had recently met a man who was the opposite of her husband. He was warm, understanding, expressive, very much in touch with his feelings and also sensitive to hers. When I enquired further, I discovered that it was the man from the previous couple.

Similarly, with responsibility, if one person begins to become overresponsible, it is as though they begin to gather up more than their share of the total responsibility available in the relationship so that the other takes less responsibility, or counters with an opposite such as incompetence or irresponsibility. If you buy a dog and then continue to bark whenever someone knocks on the door, why would the dog do anything more than sleep and eat biscuits? Yet seeing the other's incompetence or irresponsibility becomes the understandable reason for taking on more of the responsibility, and then more of the same leads to more of the same, and so on. When patterns such as these combine with personal constructs such as those elaborated above, polarizations can happen and become entrenched very quickly.

As the too-responsible person works harder and harder, the other, experiencing increasing levels of anger, disqualification, and guilt, is likely to become increasingly more incompetent or irresponsible, thus leaving the first person with an accordingly increasing amount of responsibility, etc. Where there is a construct that makes it hard for the responsible person to relinquish his position, it becomes impossible to respond to his demands to others that they be more responsible. He always seems to be there first, waiting and judging, and his definition of what constitutes an appropriate degree of responsibility always prevails. Even if he agrees to hold off for a period, he gives a clear message that he is only holding off until the other lives up to his definition of how things should be. Struggling to live up to the rigidly high, sometimes paranoid, demands of another, whose expectations always seem like the horizon (the same distance away, however fast you run), tends to perpetuate problems, in that the more it seems impossible to repay, the more the sense of obligation grows, and, like gratitude, becomes "like hatred in a mask." However, I do not assume bad intentions on the part of either side; each is usually doing whatever seems available to them at the time, given their personal constructs and the position in which they find themselves. Each side's attempted solutions to the problems they are encountering in their relationship, perceived and experienced differently as they will be by each side, have become part of a vicious cycle. It is thus important, in my opinion, to look not only at the longitudinal, intergenerational patterns, but also to consider the here-and-now, interactional determinants.

As Fisch et al. assert, "If problem formation and maintenance are seen as parts of a vicious-cycle process, in which well-intentioned solution behaviors maintain the problem, then alteration of these behaviors should interrupt the cycle and initiate resolution of the problem" (1982, p. 18). In other words, "less of the same" can lead to "less of the same," and so on. However, I have found that addressing just the interactional components of a problem without spending time working on reediting aspects of the intergenerational "biography" tends to be ineffective where the problems have become an integral part of a pattern of overresponsibility/underresponsibility that has been "handed down" through several generations.

A 40-year-old woman contacted me suffering from acute anxiety. She had recently left her husband and grown-up children and attempted to start a new life for herself, moving from the country to Sydney. Her husband had been the "boy next door," her first boyfriend, and she had married him at 18 years of age mainly, now that she looked back on it, because their families and everybody else in their small country town had expected it. She had endured 22 years of boredom. He was a kind, hardworking man, and she felt terrible that she had caused him pain. Yet she was sure that she had made the right move.

However, her immediate problem was that, every Sunday morning, her mother would telephone and subject her to an hour of criticism and demands that she should return to her "poor, unhappy husband, who loves you and has never done anything to deserve the hurt you are putting him through. Nobody could have asked for a better husband." After an hour of trying to reason with her mother, appealing to her, begging her to listen and to try to understand her point of view, she would be "a pool of liquid guilt and impotent anger on the floor beside the phone." She would drink the best part of a bottle of sherry most Sundays but, for the next two or three days, relieved that the call was over, would function quite well in the job that she had found. Then, as the week progressed, she would begin to anticipate the next call and to suffer increasing levels of anxiety.

She described her mother as a very conservative, traditional country housewife, and a domineering martyr who had, and in many ways still did, ruled the family through her migraine attacks and her endless hard work. Having explored with the woman how her present difficulties were embedded in this intergenerational context, I made a suggestion as to how she could cope with the next telephone call from her mother. As early as possible during the conversation, she was to say, calmly, without raising her voice, "I know you are upset and am sorry, it was not my intention to upset you, but I have to work this thing out for myself and I do not want to talk about it at the moment." She was not to say anything more on the matter even if she had to repeat this phrase over and over again. In no way was she to try to justify herself to her mother, to beg her, or, to in any other way try to explain her reasons for doing what she had done.

At the beginning of the next telephone call, as her mother began to apply the pressure, the woman tried what I had suggested. There was a slight pause at the other end of the line, and then it seemed her mother decided to ignore what she had heard, and she continued to demand that her daughter pull herself together and get herself "out of this silly phase." The woman repeated the phrase. In all, she used it about 15 times, far less than she had anticipated. Her mother had become rapidly less difficult, and had, for the first time, begun to express an interest in how she was coping, how she was enjoying her new job, etc. At the end of the call, instead of finishing with the usual demand that she come to her senses and remember her responsibilities, her mother wished her "all the best," told her to look after herself, and ended the conversation with "God bless you, love." In subsequent conversations, though she had to use my phrase every now and again, it rapidly became redundant as she found her mother showing an increasing level of understanding, eventually sharing that there had been times when she had dreamed of "getting away from it all." The woman then remembered what I had earlier said about how difficult it might be for her mother, having invested so much for so long in the traditional role model, to admit to herself that there might have been a different way. What her daughter had done might have uncomfortably highlighted for her the opportunities she had now lost forever.

It was important not just to have joined this woman in an overt or covert coalition against her mother such that, even though the technique in the short term might have worked, she would probably, in the long term, have felt more guilty. As Boszormenyi-Nagy and Spark observe, "Separation . . . may induce guilt feelings in the perpetrator, and guilt is the greatest obstacle to the success of genuinely autonomous emancipation" (1984, p. 32). Exploring the story of her family such that the pattern and not the parent became the problem, meant that the technique became a way of limiting *its* influence rather than of dealing more effectively with her mother.

The couple referred to earlier in this paper, who felt they had failed their son, the husband's parents, and each other, had become totally demoralized by the time they came to see me. Their youngest son, diagnosed at an early age as "hyperactive," and now 21, had always been difficult and, over the last year, had been behaving in increasingly bizarre ways, and had recently taken an overdose. It was clear that for 20 years they had seriously neglected both their marital relationship and their own personal development for the sake of the children and, more recently, for the husband's mother, whom he admitted had retained an "unhealthy power over me all throughout our married life." They talked longingly of the holiday that they had dreamed of for many years, a trip around Tasmania. It was something they planned to do as soon as all of the children were settled. After discussing with them the way that their self-neglect was part of a pattern spanning at least three generations, I suggested they seriously consider taking such a holiday within the next few weeks (the husband was a university lecturer and had several weeks holiday still to come), that they announce it rather than discuss it with, or ask permission of, their children or his mother. It was important, if they decided to take my advice, that they not justify their decision nor argue about it if any member of the family raised objections. They were just to announce that they were going because they had decided they wanted (not needed) a holiday on their own. They laughed when I ordered that they only take such a holiday if they really wanted it, rather than to obey the instructions of their therapist. Several days later they telephoned to postpone their next appointment because they would be in Tasmania. Much to their surprise, there were no objections from anybody and the youngest son had even arranged to stay with a friend while they were away.

CONCLUSION

A polarized and chronic pattern of overresponsibility and underresponsibility in a family is embedded both vertically in a historical, intergenerational tradition, and also horizontally in repetitive sequences of behavior that reflect limiting personal construct systems. Therapy for the problems that arise in such families must take into account and address both the intergenerational themes that have led to the feelings of unworthiness, obligation, guilt, etc., that are a feature of such systems, and also the here-and-now interactional patterns that serve to maintain and intensify the problems, and the constructs through which they are viewed. Through the process of reviewing and rewriting, the intergenerational transactional pattern and the personal constructs that have both caused and resulted from it can be seen as "to blame" rather than the actors within it, and thus people can be more easily persuaded to challenge the pattern through trying "less of the same" in relation to the specific problems in their current relationships. The case examples used have been chosen to highlight the themes of the paper, not to suggest that such problems can usually be substantially resolved through simple behavioral prescriptions (even though it does sometimes seem to happen), nor that it is always easy to persuade people to try approaches that totally contradict much they have believed in for many years.

A FINAL STORY

A 35-year-old woman was referred following a prolonged "depression." A hardworking wife and mother, her house obsessively clean, the only child of "strict, exemplary Irish Catholic parents," she had always been "a good girl" and had never, as far as she could remember, showed any signs of rebellion. Yet she did not feel "a good girl." She was struggling with feelings of worthlessness and failure. "I am so selfish. I have two wonderful children, even though they often give me a hard time, and my husband works so hard in order to give us a comfortable life." I shared with her my experience that most of the people who sat in my consulting room and declared themselves to be selfish had absolutely no idea about how to be so. She agreed that she basically had done nothing for herself for as far back as she could remember, and eventually accepted, intellectually at least, that it was important to be selfish sometimes, and that selfishness was only bad if it was excessive. She also accepted, though she found the idea difficult to grasp, my assurance that an increase in selfishness on her part would be of lasting benefit to her children. She agreed at the end of the session that she would consider seriously my suggestion that, during the next couple of weeks, she would leave herself open to the possibility of surprising herself by spontaneously doing something selfish, even, perhaps, a little wicked.

She returned to the next session with a smug, mischievous look. Several days after the last appointment, she had seen the children off to school, then walked back to the kitchen to do the washing up (following which it was her normal daily practice to clean the house from top to bottom). She had looked at the dishes and, to her surprise, found herself saying to them, "Damn you, you can wait till later." Without having thought about it beforehand, she knew that she was going to go to the beach. It would be the first time she had ever done this without the rest of the family. She went to her wardrobe to collect her swimsuit, but, deciding it was somewhat drab, drove to the beach and went into a shop to buy a new one. While looking at the one-piece suits, she noticed that most of the other women there, some of them around her age, and many of them more overweight than she, were buying bikinis. After some time, she finally summoned up all her courage and bought herself a bikini. Feeling extremely self-conscious, she quickly realized that nobody in the crowded shop had given her a second glance.

After a short while on the beach, she noticed that many of the women around her were only wearing the lower part of their bikinis.

" . . . and then I had this wicked thought!"

To this day, the woman's family does not know that she sunbathed topless ("My parents would be absolutely horrified if they knew."). She is no longer depressed and generally feels far more confident. She finds the children easier to handle, and her husband has become more attentive. "I have not done it again, and I probably won't. The bikini is tucked at the back of my dressing table drawer. The important thing is that I know it is there and that, if I ever wanted to, I could do it again."

EPILOGUE

We think it important to end with a warning to therapists, brief or otherwise, about the work of a somewhat dangerous therapist named Moshe Talmon. He is the author of a book *Single-Session Therapy*, the title of which is enough to send shivers down the spines of those of us who are in full-time private practice (Talmon, 1990). Intrigued by the number of clients/patients who only attend one session, and who would be defined by many frameworks and by many therapists as "drop-outs," Talmon decided to undertake some follow-up research, initially on patients from his own case load.

> In spite of my fears about what I would hear, the results of my follow-ups seemed almost too good to be true: 78 percent of the 200 patients I called said that they got what they wanted out of the single session and felt better or much better about the problem that had led them to seek therapy. (Talmon, 1990, p. 9)

He also determined, by examining the pattern of practice of upwards of 30 psychiatrists, psychologists, and social workers working in a medical center that single session therapies were not uncommon: " . . . the therapeutic orientation of the therapists had no impact on the percentage of SSTs in their total practice" (p. 7).

Subsequently, the research was extended. With two colleagues, Michael Hoyt and Robert Rosenbaum, Talmon undertook a more formal research program. Of those contacted who had attended only one session, 88% reported either "much improvement" or "improvement," 79% thought that the one session had been sufficient, and 65% had also experienced changes in areas other than those for which they had initially sought therapy.

At Talmon's request, Mordecai Kaffman, medical director of the Kibbutz Child and Family Clinic in Israel undertook a similar study. His research showed similar results.

In his book, Talmon gives comprehensive and clear guidelines on how to do effective single session therapy. The cases described show that the people who can be significantly helped in this way range from those with relatively straightforward difficulties to those who are suffering from depression, anxiety, weight problems, the aftermath of divorce, and family violence.

You can see why we consider this research to be extremely ominous. Most of us in private practice can survive reasonably well if our clients come for the five or six sessions that much research describes as being the average number of visits that people tend to make. However, if word spreads that much help can be gained from just a single session, we may have to take up cab-driving or some other part-time occupation to supplement our incomes.

A final warning. As brief therapists, we have found that it is common, particularly at workshops, to be presented with "Yes, but what if . . . " questions by our professional colleagues. For example,

"Yes, but what if she had been clinically depressed and really suicidal?"
"Yes, but what if the parents had refused to back off because the problems of their teenager were masking their marital difficulties?"
"Yes, but what if he was addicted to violent behavior?"

Such questions are often genuine attempts to understand further the principles and values of brief therapy. However, there are those times when the poser of the question is clearly making a position statement on how he or she thinks the case ought to have been diagnosed and ought to have been dealt with, rather than asking a question. A colleague has allowed us to share a story he has constructed that can be used to respond to questions that are clearly of the latter kind.

A client was rejected by his/her parents at age two and was then raised by a group of gorillas living in the slums of the dock area of San Francisco. After struggling to learn English from the fragments of newspaper left in the trash cans around the docks, he/she found him/herself struggling with issues of divided loyalties in the war between the Hispanic street gangs and the gorilla herds, feeling simultaneously the feelings of dislocation of the Hispanics and the cultural oppression experienced by the gorillas. After he came to terms with being a person and not a lesser primate, he/she crawled to a church and was systematically sexually abused by a succession of people before becoming co-dependent and adopting a lifestyle of trying to help young homeless monkeys. In therapy, we struggled with his/her active thoughts about swinging from the underneath of freeway ramps and decided not to report his/her active, serious "primate ideation" to the authorities, but chose to share our own experiences of times we have felt like eating bananas. Of course, we are unable to answer questions such as, "Yes, but what if he/she had been raised by a herd of giraffes, instead?" (Michael Durrant, 1992, personal communication)

REFERENCES

Adams, J. F., Piercy, F. P., & Jurich, J. A. (1991). Effects of solution focused therapy's "formula first session task" on compliance and outcome in family therapy. *Journal of Marital and Family Therapy, 17:* 277-290.

Adcock, C. J. (1964). *Fundamentals of psychology.* Harmondsworth, Middlesex, England: Penguin Books.

Argyle, M. (1983). *The psychology of interpersonal behaviour.* Harmondsworth, Middlesex, England: Penguin Books.

Bateson, G., Jackson, D. D., Haley, J., & Weakland, J. H. (1956). Toward a theory of schizophrenia. *Behavioral Science, 1:* 251-264.

Bem, D. J. (1965). An experimental analysis of self persuasion. *Journal of Experimental Social Psychology, 1:* 199-218.

Bem, D. J. (1968). Attitudes and self-descriptions: Another look at the behavior-attitude link. In A. G. Greenwald, T. C. Brock, & T. M. Ostrom (Eds.), *Psychological foundations of attitudes.* New York: Academic Press.

Berg, I. K. (1991). *Family preservation: A brief therapy workbook.* London: B T Press.

Berg, I. K., & Miller, S. D. (1992). *Working with the problem drinker: A solution-focused approach.* New York: W. W. Norton.

Bettinghaus, E. P., & Cody, M. J. (1987). *Persuasive communication.* New York: Holt, Rinehart & Winston.

Bodin, A., & Ferber, A. (1972). How to go beyond the use of language. In A. Ferber, M. Mendelsohn, & A. Napier (Eds.), *The book of family therapy* (pp. 272-317). Boston: Houghton Mifflin.

Bodin, A. M. (1981). The interactional view: Family therapy approaches of the Mental Research Institute. In A. Gurman & D. Kniskern (Eds.), *Handbook of family therapy* (pp. 267-309). New York: Brunner/Mazel.

Boszormenyi-Nagy, I., & Krasner, B. (1986). *Between give and take: A clinical guide to contextual therapy.* New York: Brunner/ Mazel.

Boszormenyi-Nagy, I., & Spark, G. M. (1984). *Invisible loyalties: Reciprocity in intergenerational family therapy.* New York: Brunner/ Mazel.

Brehm, J. W. (1966). *A theory of psychological reactance.* New York: Academic Press.

Breunlin, D., & Cade, B. (1981). Intervening in family systems with observer messages. *Journal of Marital and Family Therapy, 7:* 453-460.

Breunlin, D., Jones, H., & Packer, A. (1980). Therapist style in family therapy: Two contrasting case studies. *Barnardo's Social Work Papers, 9:* 7-46.

Bronowski, J. (1978). *The origins of knowledge and imagination.* New Haven, CT: Yale University Press.

Brooks, W. D., & Heath, R. W. (1989). *Speech communication.* Dubuque, IA: W. M. C. Brown Publishers.

Cacioppo, J. T., & Petty, R. E. (1979). Effects of message repetition and position on cognitive responses, recall and persuasion. *Journal of Personality and Social Psychology, 37:* 97-109.

Cade, B. (1979). The use of paradox in therapy. In S. W. Skinner (Ed.), *Family and marital psychotherapy: A critical approach* (pp. 91-105). London: Routledge & Kegan Paul.

Cade, B. (1980a). Resolving therapeutic deadlocks using a contrived team conflict. *International Journal of Family Therapy, 2:* 253-262.

Cade, B. (1980b). Strategic therapy. *Journal of Family Therapy, 2:* 89-99.

Cade, B. (1985a). Stuckness, unpredictability and change. *The Australian and New Zealand Journal of Family Therapy, 6:* 9-15.

Cade, B. (1985b). The Wizard of Oz approach to brief family therapy: An interview with Steve de Shazer. *The Australian and New Zealand Journal of Family Therapy, 6:* 95-97.

Cade, B. (1991). Unpredictability and change: A holographic metaphor. In G. Weeks (Ed.), *Promoting change through paradoxical therapy* (pp. 28-59). New York: Brunner/Mazel.

Cade, B. (1992a). A response by any other. . . . *Journal of Family Therapy, 14:* 163-169.

Cade, B. (1992b). I am an unashamed expert. *Context: A News Magazine of Family Therapy, 11:* 30-31.

Cade, B., & Southgate, P. (1979). Honesty is the best policy. *Journal of Family Therapy, 1:* 23-31.

Cade, B. W., Speed, B., & Seligman, P. (1986). Working in teams: The pros and cons. In F. W. Kaslow (Ed.), *Supervision and training: Models, dilemmas, and challenges* (pp. 105-117). New York: Haworth.

Capra, F. (1976). *The Tao of physics*. London: Fontana/Collins.
Card, O. S. (1987). *Wyrms*. London: Arrow Books.
Chomsky, N. (1972). *Language and mind*. New York: Harcourt, Brace, Jovanovich.
Chomsky, N. (1975). *Reflections on language*. New York: Pantheon.
Combs, G., & Freedman, J. (1990). *Symbol, story and ceremony: Using metaphor in individual and family therapy*. New York: W. W. Norton.
Cornwell, M., & Pearson, R. (1981). Cotherapy teams and one-way screen in family therapy training and practice. *Family Process, 20:* 199–209.
Coyne, J. C. (1985). Toward a theory of frames and reframing: The social nature of frames. *Journal of Marital and Family Therapy, 11:* 337–344.
Crawford, J., Kippax, S., Onyx, J., Gault, U., & Benton, P. (1992). *Emotion and gender: Constructing meaning from memory*. London: Sage.
de Bono, E. (1971). *The mechanism of mind*. Harmondsworth, Middlesex: Penguin Books.
de Shazer, S. (1980). Brief family therapy: A metaphorical task. *Journal of Marital and Family Therapy, 6:* 471–476.
de Shazer, S. (1982). *Patterns of brief family therapy: An ecosystemic approach*. New York: Guilford.
de Shazer, S. (1985). *Keys to solution in brief therapy*. New York: W. W. Norton.
de Shazer, S. (1988). *Clues: Investigating solutions in brief therapy*. New York: W. W. Norton.
de Shazer, S. (1991). *Putting difference to work*. New York: W. W. Norton.
de Shazer, S., & Molnar, A. (1984). Four useful interventions in brief family therapy. *Journal of Marital and Family Therapy, 10:* 297–304.
de Shazer, S., Berg, I. K., Lipchik, E., Nunnally, E., Molnar, A., Gingerich, W., & Weiner-Davis, M. (1986). Brief therapy: Focused solution development. *Family Process, 25:* 207–222.
Dell, P. F. (1981). Some irreverent thoughts on paradox. *Family Process, 20:* 37–51.
Dolan, Y. M. (1991). *Resolving sexual abuse: Solution-focused therapy and Ericksonian hypnosis for adult survivors*. New York: W. W. Norton.
Duncan, B. L. (1992). Strategic therapy, eclecticism, and the therapeutic relationship. *Journal of Marital and Family Therapy, 18:* 17–24.
Dunlap, K. (1928). A revision of the fundamental law of habit formation. *Science, 57:* 360–362.
Dunlap, K. (1930). Repetition in the breaking of habits. *Science Monthly, 30:* 66–70.

Eco, U. (1983). *The name of the rose.* London: Picador.

Erickson, M. H. (1954). Pseudo-orientation in time as a hypnothera-peutic procedure. *Journal of Clinical and Experimental Hypnosis, 2:* 261–283.

Erickson, M. H., & Rossi, E. L. (1979). *Hypnotherapy: An exploratory casebook.* New York: Irvington.

Erickson, M. H., Rossi, E. L., & Rossi, S. I. (1976). *Hypnotic realities: The induction of clinical hypnosis and forms of indirect suggestion.* New York: Irvington.

Fane, J. (1988). *Cautionary tales for women.* England: Hamish Hamilton & St. Georges Press.

Feyerabend, P. (1978). *Against method: Outline of an anarchistic theory of knowledge.* London: Verso.

Fisch, R., Weakland, J. H., & Segal, L. (1982). *The tactics of change: Doing therapy briefly.* San Francisco: Jossey-Bass.

Fisher, L., Anderson, A., & Jones, J. E. (1981). Types of paradoxical intervention and indications/contraindications for use in clinical practice. *Family Process, 20:* 25–35.

Flaskas, C. (1992). A reframe by any other name: On the process of reframing in strategic, Milan and analytic therapy. *Journal of Family Therapy, 14:* 145–161.

Frankl, V. (1969). *The doctor and the soul: From psychotherapy to logotherapy.* London: Souvenir Press.

Frankl, V. (1970). *Psychotherapy and existentialism: Selected papers on logotherapy.* London: Souvenir Press.

Fransella, F., & Bannister, D. (1977). *A manual for repertory grid technique.* London: Academic Press.

Frude, N., & Dowling, E. (1980). A follow-up analysis of family therapy clients. *Journal of Family Therapy, 2:* 149–161.

Furman, B., & Ahola, T. (1992). *Solution talk: Hosting therapeutic conversations.* New York: W. W. Norton.

Gendlin, E. T. (1973). A phenomenology of emotions: Anger. In D. Carr & E. Casey (Eds.), *Explorations in phenomenology.* The Hague, Netherlands: Matinus Nijhoff.

Gentry, D. (1973). Directive therapy techniques in the treatment of migraine headaches: A case study. *Psychotherapy: Theory, Research, Practice, 10:* 308–311.

Goolishian, H. A., & Anderson, H. (1992). Strategy and intervention versus nonintervention: A matter of theory? *Journal of Marital and Family Therapy, 18:* 5–15.

Greenberg, G. S. (1977). The family interactional perspective: A study and examination of the work of Don D. Jackson. *Family Process, 16:* 385–412.

Greenberg, G. S. (1980). Problem focused brief family interactional psychotherapy. In L. R. Wolberg & M. L. Aronson (Eds.), *Group and family therapy* (pp. 307–322). New York: Brunner/Mazel.

Grinder, J., & Bandler, R. (1981). *Trance formations*. Moab, UT: Real People Press.

Grube, J., Greenstein, T., Rankin, W., & Kearney, K. (1977). Behavior change following self-confrontation: A test of the value-mediation hypothesis. *Journal of Personality and Social Psychology, 35:* 212–216.

Haley, J. (1963). *Strategies of psychotherapy*. New York: Grune & Stratton.

Haley, J. (1967a). Toward a theory of pathological systems. In G. H. Zuk & I. Boszormenyi-Nagy (Eds.), *Family therapy and disturbed families* (pp. 11–27). Palo Alto, CA: Science and Behavior Books.

Haley, J. (1973). *Uncommon therapy: The psychiatric techniques of Milton H. Erickson*. New York: W. W. Norton.

Haley, J. (1976). *Problem solving therapy*. San Francisco: Jossey-Bass.

Haley, J. (1980a). How to be a marriage therapist without knowing practically anything. *Journal of Marital and Family Therapy, 6:* 385–391.

Haley, J. (1980b). *Leaving home*. New York: McGraw-Hill.

Haley, J. (Ed.) (1967b). *Advanced techniques of hypnosis and therapy: Selected papers of Milton H. Erickson*. New York: Grune & Stratton.

Haley, J. (Ed.) (1985). *Conversations with Milton H. Erickson, M.D.* New York: Triangle Press.

Harré, R., & Secord, P. F. (1972). *The explanation of social behavior*. Oxford: Basil Blackwell.

Harrison, J. (1986). *Sundog*. Harmondsworth, Middlesex: Penguin.

Hoffman, L. (1981). *Foundations of family therapy*. New York: Basic.

Jackson, D. D. (1975). The question of family homeostasis. *Psychiatric Quarterly Supplement, 31:* 79–90.

Kearney, P., O'Reilly-Byrne, N., & Colgan-McCarthy, I. (1989). Just metaphors: Marginal illuminations in a colonial retreat. *Family Therapy Case Studies, 4:* 17–31.

Keith, D. V., & Whitaker, C. A. (1985). Failure: Our bold companion. In S. B. Coleman (Ed.), *Failures in family therapy* (pp. 8–23). New York: Guilford.

Kelly, G. (1955). *The psychology of personal constructs*. New York: W. W. Norton.

Kelly, G. (1969). The autobiography of a theory. In B. Maher (Ed.), *Clinical psychology and personality: The selected papers of George Kelly*. New York: Wiley.

Kiesler, C. A. (1971). *The psychology of commitment: Experiments linking behavior to belief*. New York: Academic Press.

Kleckner, T., Frank, L., Bland, C., Amendt, J. H., & duRee Bryant, R. (1992). The myth of the unfeeling strategic therapist. *Journal of Marital and Family Therapy, 18:* 41–51.

Koestler, A. (1975). *The act of creation.* London: Picador.

Kowalski, K., & Kral, R. (1989). The geometry of solution: Using the scaling technique. *Family Therapy Case Studies, 4*(1): 59–66.

Kundera, M. (1990). *Immortality.* New York: Grove Weidenfeld.

Laing, R. D. (1965). *The divided self.* Harmondsworth, Middlesex: Penguin Books.

Lankton, S., & Lankton, C. (1983). *The answer within: A clinical framework of Ericksonian hypnotherapy.* New York: Brunner/Mazel.

Madanes, C. (1981a). Family therapy in the treatment of psychosomatic illness in childhood and adolescence. In L. R. Wolberg & M. L. Aronson (Eds.), *Group and family therapy* (pp. 219–234). New York: Brunner/Mazel.

Madanes, C. (1981b). *Strategic family therapy.* San Francisco: Jossey-Bass.

Madanes, C. (1984). *Behind the one-way mirror: Advances in the practice of strategic therapy.* San Francisco: Jossey-Bass.

Markowitz, L. M. (1992). Around the network. *Family Therapy Networker, 16:* 12–14.

McGregor, H. (1990). Conceptualising male violence against female partners. *The Australian and New Zealand Journal of Family Therapy, 11:* 65–70.

McGuire, W. J. (1964). Inducing resistance to persuasion: Some contemporary approaches. In L. Berkowitz (Ed.), *Advances in experimental social psychology* (vol. 1). New York: Academic Press.

Miller, G. R. (1980). On being persuaded: Some basic distinctions. In M. E. Roloff & G. R. Miller (Eds.), *Persuasion: New directions in theory and research* (pp. 11–28). Beverly Hills, CA: Sage.

Miller, S. D. (1992). The symptoms of solution. *Journal of Strategic and Systemic Therapies, 11:* 1–11.

Minuchin, S., & Fishman, H. C. (1981). *Family therapy techniques.* Cambridge, MA: Harvard University Press.

Mischel, W. (1968). *Personality and assessment.* New York: Wiley.

Molnar, A., & de Shazer, S. (1987). Solution-focused therapy: Toward the identification of therapeutic tasks. *Journal of Marital and Family Therapy, 13:* 349–358.

Mozdzierz, G., Maccitelli, F., & Lisiecki, J. (1976). The paradox in psychotherapy: An Adlerian perspective. *Journal of Individual Psychology, 32:* 169–184.

Nisbett, R. E., & Schachter, S. (1966). Cognitive manipulation of pain. *Journal of Experimental Social Psychology, 2:* 227–236.

Nunnally, J. C., & Bobren, H. M. (1959). Variables governing the willingness to receive communications on mental health. *Journal of Personality, 27:* 275–290.

O'Hanlon, W. H. (1982). Strategic pattern intervention. *Journal of Strategic and Systemic Therapies, 1:* 26–33.

O'Hanlon, W. H. (1987). *Taproots: Underlying principles of Milton H. Erickson's therapy and hypnosis.* New York: W. W. Norton.

O'Hanlon, W. H. (1990). A grand unified theory for brief therapy: Putting problems in context. In J. K. Zeig & S. G. Gilligan (Eds.), *Brief therapy: Myths, methods and metaphors* (pp. 78–89). New York: Brunner/Mazel.

O'Hanlon, W. H. (1991). Not strategic, not systemic: Still clueless after all these years. *Journal of Strategic and Systemic Therapies, 10:* 105–109.

O'Hanlon, W. H., & Martin, M. (1992). *Solution-oriented hypnosis: An Ericksonian approach.* New York: W. W. Norton.

O'Hanlon, W. H., & Weiner-Davis, M. (1989). *In search of solutions: A new direction in psychotherapy.* New York: W. W. Norton.

O'Hanlon, W. H., & Wilk, J. (1987). *Shifting contexts: The generation of effective psychotherapy.* New York: Guilford.

Palazzoli, M. S. (1974). *Self starvation: From the intrapsychic to the transpersonal approach to anorexia nervosa.* London: Chaucer Publishing.

Palazzoli, M. S. (1981). Comments on "Some irreverent thoughts on paradox." *Family Process, 20:* 37–51.

Palazzoli, M. S., Boscolo, L., Cecchin, G., & Prata, G. (1974). The treatment of children through brief therapy of their parents. *Family Process, 13:* 429–442.

Palazzoli, M. S., Boscolo, L., Cecchin, G., & Prata, G. (1975, Aug.). *Paradox and counterparadox: A new model for the therapy of the family in schizophrenic transition.* Paper presented at the Fifth International Symposium on the Psychotherapy of Schizophrenia, Oslo, Norway.

Palazzoli, M. S., Boscolo, L., Cecchin, G., & Prata, G. (1978). *Paradox and counterparadox.* New York: Jason Aronson.

Palazzoli, M. S., Boscolo, L., Cecchin, G., & Prata, G. (1980a). Hypothesizing-circularity-neutrality: Three guidelines for the conduct of the session. *Family Process, 19:* 3–12.

Palazzoli, M. S., Boscolo, L., Cecchin, G., & Prata, G. (1980b). The problem of the referring person. *Journal of Marital and Family Therapy, 6:* 3–9.

Palazzoli, M. S.; Cirillo, S., Selvini, M., & Sorrentino, A. M. (1989). *Family games: General models of psychotic processes in the family.* New York: W. W. Norton.

Papp, P. (1980). The Greek chorus and other techniques of family therapy. *Family Process, 19:* 45–58.

Papp, P. (1983). *The process of change.* New York: Guilford.

Parsons, B. V., & Alexander, J. F. (1973). Short term family intervention: A therapy outcome study. *Journal of Consulting and Clinical Psychology, 41:* 195–201.

Perloff, R. M., & Brock, T. C. (1980). "And thinking makes it so":

Cognitive responses to persuasion. In M. E. Roloff & G. R. Miller (Eds.), *Persuasion: New directions in theory and research* (pp. 67–99). Beverly Hills, CA: Sage.

Petty, R. E., & Cacioppo, J. T. (1977). Forewarning, cognitive responding, and resistance to persuasion. *Journal of Personality and Social Psychology, 35:* 645–655.

Rabkin, R. (1977). *Strategic psychotherapy: Brief and symptomatic treatment.* New York: Basic.

Rohrbaugh, M., Tennen, H., Press, S., & White, L. (1981). Compliance, defiance and therapeutic paradox. *American Journal of Orthopsychiatry, 51:* 454–467.

Rohrbaugh, M., Tennen, H., Press, S., White, L., Raskin, P., & Pickering, M. (1977, Aug.). *Paradoxical strategies in psychotherapy.* Paper presented at the annual meeting of American Psychological Association, San Francisco, California.

Rokeach, M. (1968). *Beliefs, attitudes and values.* San Francisco: Jossey-Bass.

Romain, J. (1973). *Verdun.* St. Albans, England: Mayflower Books.

Rose, S. (1976). *The conscious brain.* Harmondsworth, Middlesex: Penguin Books.

Rosen, J. (1953). *Direct psychoanalysis.* New York: Irvington.

Rosen, S. (1982). *My voice will go with you: The teaching tales of Milton H. Erickson, M.D.* New York: W. W. Norton.

Rosenhan, D. L. (1973). On being sane in insane places. *Science, 179:* 250–258.

Rosenthal, R. (1966). *Experimenter effects in behavioral research.* New York: Appleton-Century-Crofts.

Rosenthal, R., & Jacobson, L. (1968). *Pygmalion in the classroom.* New York: Holt, Rinehart & Winston.

Rossi, E. L. (Ed.) (1980). *The collected papers of Milton Erickson.* New York: Irvington.

Rossi, E. L., Ryan, M. O., & Sharp, F. A. (1983). *Healing in hypnosis: The seminars, workshops and lectures of Milton H. Erickson, Volume 1.* New York: Irvington.

Russell, P. (1979). *The brain book.* London: Routledge & Kegan Paul.

Sartre, J. P. (1965). *Nausea.* Harmondsworth, Middlesex: Penguin Books.

Schachter, S., & Singer, J. E. (1962). Cognitive, social, and physiological determinants of emotional state. *Psychological Review, 69:* 379–399.

Scheflen, A. E. (1978). Susan smiled: On explanation in family therapy. *Family Process, 17:* 59–68.

Scheflen, A. E. (1981). *Levels of schizophrenia.* New York: Brunner/Mazel.

Schultz, D. (1990). *Theories of personality.* Pacific Grove, CA: Brooks/Cole.

Shannon, C. E., & Weaver, W. (1949). *The mathematical theory of communication.* Urbana: University of Illinois Press.

Speed, B. (1984a). Family therapy: An update. *Association for Child Psychology and Psychiatry Newsletter, 6:* 2–14.

Speed, B. (1984b). How really real is real? *Family Process, 23:* 511–520.

Speed, B. (1991). Reality exists O.K.? An argument against constructivism and social constructionism. *Journal of Family Therapy, 13:* 395–409.

Speed, B., Seligman, P., Kingston, P., & Cade, B. (1982). A team approach to therapy. *Journal of Family Therapy, 4:* 271–284.

Spencer-Brown, G. (1979). *Laws of form.* New York: E. P. Dutton.

Stanton, M. D. (1981). Strategic approaches to family therapy. In A. Gurman & D. Kniskern (Eds.), *Handbook of family therapy* (pp. 361–402). New York: Brunner/Mazel.

Stephens, B. J. (1987). Cheap thrills and humble pie: The adolescence of female suicide attempters. *Suicide and Life Threatening Behavior, 17:* 107–118.

Storms, M. D., & Nisbett, R. E. (1970). Insomnia and the attribution process. *Journal of Personality and Social Psychology, 16:* 319–328.

Strauss, A. L. (1977). *Mirrors and masks: The search for identity.* London: Martin Robertson & Co.

Talmon, M. (1990). *Single-session therapy.* San Francisco: Jossey-Bass.

Teismann, M. W. (1979). Jealousy: Systemic, problem-solving therapy with couples. *Family Process, 18:* 151–160.

Tennen, H. (1977, Aug.). *Perspectives on paradox: Applications and explanations.* Paper presented at the annual meeting of the American Psychological Association, San Francisco, California.

Von Neuman, J., & Morgenstern, O. (1944). *The theory of games and economic behavior.* Princeton, NJ: Princeton University Press.

Waddington, C. H. (1977). *Tools for thought.* St. Albans, England: Paladin.

Wallas, L. (1985). *Stories for the third ear: Using hypnotic fables in psychotherapy.* New York: W. W. Norton.

Walter, J. L., & Peller, J. E. (1992). *Becoming solution-focused in brief therapy.* New York: Brunner/Mazel.

Watzlawick, P. (1976). *How real is real?* New York: Random House.

Watzlawick, P. (1978). *The language of change: Elements of therapeutic communication.* New York: Basic.

Watzlawick, P. (1983). *The situation is hopeless, but not serious.* New York: W. W. Norton.

Watzlawick, P. (Ed.) (1984). *The invented reality.* New York: W. W. Norton.

Watzlawick, P., Beavin, J. H., & Jackson, D. D. (1967). *Pragmatics of human communication.* New York: W. W. Norton.

Watzlawick, P., Weakland, J. H., & Fisch, R. (1974). *Change: Principles of problem formation and problem resolution.* New York: W. W. Norton.

Weakland, J., & Jordan, L. (1990). Working briefly with reluctant clients: Child protective services as an example. *Family Therapy Case Studies, 5:* 51–68.

Weakland, J. H., Fisch, R., Watzlawick, P., & Bodin, A. (1974). Brief therapy: Focused problem resolution. *Family Process, 13:* 141–168.

Weeks, G. (1977). Toward a dialectical approach to intervention. *Human Development, 20:* 277–292.

Weeks, G., & L'Abate, L. (1978). A bibliography of paradoxical methods in psychotherapy of family systems. *Family Process, 17:* 95–98.

Weeks, G., & L'Abate, L. (1982). *Paradoxical psychotherapy: Theory and practice with individuals, couples and families.* New York: Brunner/Mazel.

Wegner, D. M., Vallacher, R. R., Macomber, G., Wood, R., & Arps, K. (1984). The emergence of action. *Journal of Personality and Social Psychology, 46:* 269–279.

Weiner, N. (1948). *Cybernetics or control and communication in the animal and the machines.* New York: Wiley.

Weiner-Davies, M., de Shazer, S., & Gingerich, W. J. (1987). Building on pretreatment change to construct the therapeutic solution: An exploratory study. *Journal of Marital and Family Therapy, 13:* 359–363.

Welwood, J. (1982). The holographic paradigm and the structure of experience. In K. Wilber (Ed.), *The holographic paradigm and other paradoxes* (pp. 127–135). Boulder, CO: Shambhala.

White, M. (1988). The externalizing of the problem and the re-authoring of lives and relationships. *Dulwich Centre Newsletter,* Summer: 3–21.

White, M., & Epston, D. (1990). *Narrative means to therapeutic ends.* New York: W. W. Norton.

Whitehead, A. N., & Russell, B. (1910–13). *Principia mathematica.* Cambridge, England: Cambridge University Press.

Yates, J. (1958). The application of learning theory to the treatment of tics. *Journal of Abnormal and Social Psychology, 56:* 175–182.

Zeig, J. (1980). *A teaching seminar with Milton H. Erickson, M.D.* New York: Brunner/Mazel.

Zukav, G. (1979). *The dancing Wu-Li masters.* London: Fontana Paperbacks.

INDEX

195